PUBLIC HEALTH IN THE 21ST CENTURY

AIR TRAVEL AND COMMUNICABLE DISEASES

U.S. PREPAREDNESS, PLANNING AND CHALLENGES

PUBLIC HEALTH IN THE 21ST CENTURY

Additional books in this series can be found on Nova's website
under the Series tab.

Additional e-books in this series can be found on Nova's website
under the eBooks tab.

PUBLIC HEALTH IN THE 21ST CENTURY

AIR TRAVEL AND COMMUNICABLE DISEASES

U.S. PREPAREDNESS, PLANNING AND CHALLENGES

GERALD VASQUEZ
EDITOR

nova publishers
New York

Library of Congress Cataloging-in-Publication Data

ISBN: 978-1-53610-188-1

Published by Nova Science Publishers, Inc. † New York

CONTENTS

PREFACE

Past communicable diseases, such as the recent Ebola epidemic, have resulted in many deaths and highlight the potential economic cost of disruptions to air travel and the U.S. and global economies. This book examines the extent to which selected U.S. airports and airlines have plans for responding to communicable disease threats from abroad and to which a national aviation-preparedness plan guides preparedness; and the challenges that U.S. airports and airlines have faced when responding to threats and any actions taken to address them.

In: Air Travel and Communicable Diseases
Editor: Gerald Vasquez
ISBN: 978-1-53610-188-1

Chapter 1

AIR TRAVEL AND COMMUNICABLE DISEASES: COMPREHENSIVE FEDERAL PLAN NEEDED FOR U.S. AVIATION SYSTEM'S PREPAREDNESS*

United States Government Accountability Office

WHY GAO DID THIS STUDY

Past communicable diseases, such as the recent Ebola epidemic, have resulted in many deaths and highlight the potential economic cost of disruptions to air travel and the U.S. and global economies.

GAO was asked to review the preparedness of the U.S. aviation system to respond to communicable diseases. This report examines (1) the extent to which selected U.S. airports and airlines have plans for responding to communicable disease threats from abroad and to which a national aviation-preparedness plan guides preparedness, and (2) the challenges that U.S. airports and airlines have faced when responding to threats and any actions taken to address them.

GAO reviewed available documents and interviewed representatives from 14 U.S. international airports—selected to reflect a range of activities and facilities—and the 3 major U.S. airlines. GAO also reviewed applicable

* This is an edited, reformatted and augmented version of a United States Government Accountability Office, Publication No. GAO-16-127, dated December 2015.

federal requirements and international obligations and guidance for U.S. airports and airlines, and interviewed officials and reviewed documents from federal agencies and aviation stakeholder groups.

What GAO Recommends

GAO recommends that DOT work with relevant stakeholders, such as the Department of Health and Human Services, to develop a national aviation-preparedness plan for communicable diseases. DOT agrees a plan is needed, but suggests public health agencies lead the effort. GAO continues to believe the recommendation is correctly directed to DOT, as discussed in this report.

What GAO Found

All of the 14 airports and 3 airlines GAO reviewed have plans for responding to communicable disease threats from abroad, although the United States lacks a comprehensive national aviation-preparedness plan aimed at preventing and containing the spread of diseases through air travel. U.S. airports and airlines are not required to have individual preparedness plans, and no federal agency tracks which airports and airlines have them. Consequently, it is not clear the extent to which all U.S. airports and airlines have such plans. The plans GAO reviewed generally addressed the high-level components that GAO identified as common among applicable federal and international guidance, such as establishment of an incident command center and activation triggers for a response. GAO identified these components to provide a basis for assessing the breadth of the plans. The plans GAO reviewed for each airport were developed by, or in collaboration with, relevant airport stakeholders, such as Centers for Disease Control and Prevention's (CDC) airport staff. As provided in Annex 9, the Chicago Convention, an international aviation treaty to which the United States is a signatory, obligates member states to develop a national aviation-preparedness plan for communicable disease outbreaks. The Department of Transportation (DOT) and CDC officials contend that some elements of such a plan already exist, including plans at individual airports. However, FAA has reported that individual airport plans are often intended to handle one or two flights with arriving passengers, rather than an epidemic, which may require involvement from multiple airports on a national level. Most importantly, a national aviation-preparedness plan would provide airports and airlines with an adaptable and scalable framework with which to align their individual plans—to help ensure that individual airport and airline plans work in accordance with one another. DOT and CDC officials agree that a national plan could add value. Such a plan would provide a mechanism for the public-health and aviation sectors to coordinate to more effectively prevent and control a communicable disease threat while minimizing unnecessary disruptions to the national aviation system.

Aviation stakeholders GAO spoke with identified multiple challenges in responding to communicable disease threats and actions they took or would take in response. For example, airline and airport representatives told GAO they sometimes experienced difficulties sharing timely and accurate information about threats, and some reported that they improved communication by developing tools, such as standardized forms, to collect and share relevant information. Employees at aviation services firms that GAO spoke with—including contract workers who clean aircraft—raised concerns about the availability of training and access to equipment to control exposure to communicable diseases. Some airports GAO reviewed developed additional mechanisms to ensure adequate training and preparation during the Ebola threat. A national aviation-preparedness plan could serve as the basis for testing communication mechanisms among responders to ensure those mechanisms are effective prior to a communicable disease outbreak as well as to provide the basis for ensuring that airport and airline staff receive appropriate training and equipment to reduce their risk of exposure to communicable diseases during an outbreak.

ABBREVIATIONS

ACI	Airport Council International
AEP	airport-emergency plans
CAPSCA	Collaborative Arrangement for the Prevention and Management of Public Health Events in Civil Aviation
CARE	Check and Report Ebola kit
CBP	U.S. Customs and Border Protection
CDC	Centers for Disease Control and Prevention
CDRP	communicable-disease response plan

Chicago Convention	Convention on International Civil Aviation
DHS	Department of Homeland Security
DOT	Department of Transportation
FAA	Federal Aviation Administration
HEPA	high-efficiency particulate air
HHS	Department of Health and Human Services
HIV	human immunodeficiency virus
IATA	International Air Transport Association
ICAO	International Civil Aviation Organization
IHR	International Health Regulations
MERS	Middle East Respiratory Syndrome
MOU	memorandum of understanding
OSHA	Occupational Safety and Health Administration
PPD-8	Presidential Policy Directive 8
RBBS	Risk-Based Border Strategy
SARPs	standards and recommended practices
SARS	severe acute respiratory syndrome
TB	tuberculosis
WHO	World Health Organization

* * *

December 16, 2015

The Honorable Rick Larsen
Ranking Member
Subcommittee on Aviation
Committee on Transportation and Infrastructure
House of Representatives

Dear Mr. Larsen:

In 2014, almost 52-million international air travelers entered the United States, and the Federal Aviation Administration (FAA) expects that number to continue to increase as the global economy continues to develop. The Ebola epidemic in West Africa in 2014 and 2015 renewed concerns about the spread of communicable diseases through air travel. More than any other mode of transportation, air travel creates the potential for an infection to move quickly from one part of the world to another.[1] In response to Ebola there were proposals in the United States to restrict travel and trade to and from affected countries, although public health officials advised permitting travel to allow access to medical supplies and qualified personnel to contain the epidemic. While deaths and illnesses may be the most visible effect of an outbreak, communicable disease threats also create economic costs. In the case of the 2003 severe acute respiratory syndrome (SARS) epidemic, for example, the International Air Transport Association (IATA) estimated the overall cost at $33 billion of global gross domestic product in 2003. North American airline revenue losses alone were estimated at $1 billion, while Asia Pacific airlines lost an estimated $6 billion.[2]

We have found—in lessons learned from the response to the 2009 H1N1 influenza pandemic[3]—that interagency planning and exercises build formal networks and informal relationships that are valuable during a response.[4] Further, in the aviation area, international guidance for aviation stakeholders—including guidance for civil aviation authorities such as FAA—points to the importance of preparedness plans for communicable disease threats, with recommendations designed to reduce exposure to the disease and improve the response to health-related emergencies by establishing mechanisms for rapid decision-making and action.[5]

In light of recurring communicable disease threats, the continued growth in international air travel, and the need to prepare for future threats, you asked us to review issues related to the preparedness of the U.S. aviation system to respond to pandemics and other health crises. This report examines (1) the extent to which selected airports and airlines have preparedness plans to respond to communicable disease threats from abroad and the extent to which a national aviation-preparedness plan guides preparedness, and (2) what challenges U.S. airports and airlines, including their contractors, have faced when responding to communicable disease threats and any actions they have taken to respond to those challenges.

To conduct this work, we identified and reviewed applicable federal requirements, international obligations, as well as federal and international guidance for U.S. airports and airlines with international air traffic. We interviewed officials and reviewed available documents from five federal departments that represent the key federal departments with responsibilities for preparing for and responding to communicable disease threats from abroad—the Departments of Transportation (DOT), Health and Human Services (HHS), Homeland Security (DHS), State, and Labor and their relevant components, including DOT's Federal Aviation Administration (FAA), HHS's Centers for

Disease Control and Prevention (CDC), DHS's U.S. Customs and Border Protection (CBP), and Labor's Occupational Safety and Health Administration (OSHA). We identified high-level components that were common among applicable federal and international guidance, as well as corroborating information collected from aviation stakeholders whom we spoke with. Then, we developed a list of high-level components for airport and airline communicable-disease preparedness plans to provide a basis for assessing the breadth of the plans. We compared these components against the available plans collected from 14 airports and three airlines that we selected for review during our study. We did not evaluate the plans for sufficiency or level of preparedness. We selected for review 14 airports that met one or more of our selection criteria, which included being a large hub airport[6] with CDC staff on-site; receiving the largest and second largest number of international passengers from at least one of five world regions; having enhanced passenger entry-screening procedures in place for Ebola; and having experience with a confirmed Ebola case. We selected for review the three U.S. airlines that handle the largest quantity of international travelers.[7] In addition to reviewing the plans, we administered a questionnaire to each of the 14 airport operators on preparedness at their airport, such as the plans and procedures they have in place for a variety of circumstances. We interviewed a range of stakeholders to discuss preparedness plans and potential opportunities to improve preparedness, as well as to identify challenges airports and airlines have faced in responding to communicable disease threats, including Ebola, and actions stakeholders have taken to address those challenges. These stakeholders include representatives from the 14 selected airports and their local airport stakeholders—such as first responders, local public health officials, CBP officials, and CDC officials, if applicable; the three selected U.S. airlines; airport, airline, and flight attendant industry associations;[8] the International Civil Aviation Organization (ICAO); the labor union representing airport- and airline-service workers; and contracted aviation-services employers and their employees.[9] We also identified challenges and actions through our attendance at an ICAO global symposium. Additional detail on the scope and methodology of our review is contained in appendix I.

We conducted this performance audit from November 2014 to December 2015 in accordance with generally accepted government auditing standards. Those standards require that we plan and perform the audit to obtain sufficient, appropriate evidence to provide a reasonable basis for our findings and conclusions based on our audit objectives. We believe that the evidence obtained provides a reasonable basis for our findings and conclusions based on our audit objectives.

BACKGROUND

A number of communicable disease threats have raised concern regarding international transmission and travel since the 2003 SARS epidemic, which was the first major new disease of the 21st century, according to the World Health Organization (WHO) of the United Nations. WHO described that 2003 epidemic as a watershed event, because it revealed how much the world had changed in terms of the impact that communicable diseases can have in a highly mobile and closely interconnected world.[10] Figure 1 provides information about major communicable disease epidemics since 2002.

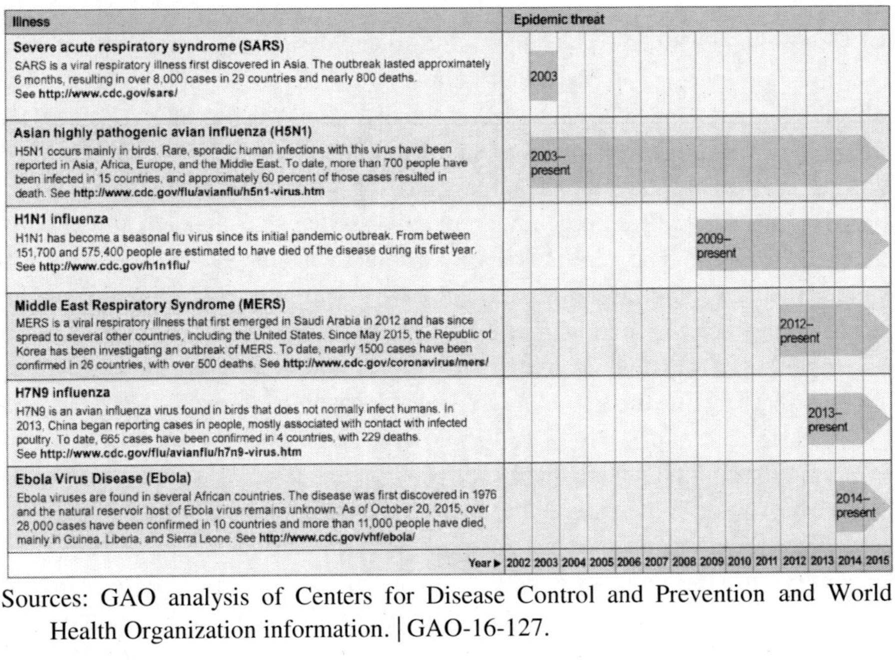

Sources: GAO analysis of Centers for Disease Control and Prevention and World Health Organization information. | GAO-16-127.

Figure 1. Major Epidemic Threats since 2002.

The International Health Regulations (IHR) are an international agreement of the World Health Assembly, the governing body of WHO, and were originally adopted by the Assembly in 1969 to address certain disease threats.

The IHR have evolved since then in response to the growth in international travel and trade and the emergence of international disease threats. Most recently, the IHR were revised in 2005 following the SARS epidemic.[11] WHO implements and oversees the IHR and—together with its partners, such as the International Civil Aviation Organization (ICAO)—helps member states build response capacities.

ICAO takes a key role in coordinating the international aviation response to public health risks.[12] Through the IHR, WHO member states have agreed to build core capacities at designated ports of entry,[13] such as airports, to limit the spread of public health risks—such as communicable disease threats—while at the same time minimizing any unnecessary interference with travel and trade.

ICAO develops international standards and recommended practices (SARPs) for civil aviation systems, in cooperation with its member states and global aviation organizations.[14] Member states, including the United States, are obligated to establish regulations or take other appropriate steps to implement the ICAO standards within their own civil aviation systems.[15] In the United States, different agencies are responsible for different aspects of the civil aviation system, as discussed below. The SARPs include some health-related standards and recommended practices based on the most recent IHR obligations. To encourage member states to comply with these health-related SARPs, ICAO has developed a template for the development of national aviation public-health emergency-preparedness plans, which are obligations under the IHR.[16] The Collaborative Arrangement for the Prevention and Management of Public Health Events in Civil Aviation (CAPSCA) also works to bring together international, regional, national, and local organizations to develop a coordinated approach to preparedness and response. Other international organizations, notably Airports Council International (ACI) and IATA, also provide assistance to airports and airlines, respectively, in preparing for communicable disease threats.

In the United States, a number of federal agencies, aviation stakeholders, and others have roles and responsibilities in preparing for, assessing, and responding to communicable disease threats in the aviation system. Each of the federal agencies involved in preparing for or responding to communicable disease threats from abroad have a different mission, including those described below, that affects their responsibilities for protecting against communicable disease threats. DHS and HHS are the lead agencies in a response to a communicable disease threat, and other federal agencies provide support as necessary.

- Within DHS, CBP aims to safeguard America's borders thereby protecting the public from dangerous people and materials while enhancing the nation's global economic competitiveness by enabling legitimate trade and travel. CBP officials at ports of entry, including airports, conduct the primary inspection of arriving international travelers and have authority to permit or deny admission to the United States.[17]
- Within HHS, CDC has defined its mission as protecting America from health, safety, and security threats, both foreign and domestic. With its partners, such as CBP, CDC responds to sick travelers who arrive in the United States at major airports, seaports, or land border crossings, when warranted. CDC alerts travelers about disease outbreaks and steps they can take to protect themselves. CDC also has the authority to quarantine passengers traveling from foreign countries, if necessary, to protect the general population and respond to disease threats to the United States.[18]
- Within DOT, FAA is responsible for safety of flight in the United States and the safe and efficient movement of air traffic in the national airspace system, as well as for the safety of U.S. airlines, other U.S. operators, and FAA-certificated air crews worldwide. As part of this responsibility, the agency regulates and certificates airports, airlines, and airmen and provides guidance through advisory circulars and other means.
- Within the Department of Labor, OSHA aims to assure safe and healthful working conditions for working men and women by setting and enforcing standards and by providing training, outreach, education, compliance, and assistance.[19]
- The Department of State (State) has the authority to grant visas, which allow foreign citizens to travel to a U.S. port of entry (generally an airport) and request permission to enter the United States.[20]

Depending on location and threat, these agencies along with aviation stakeholders and their partners—including local public health authorities,[21] first responders, contracted aviation-services firms, and others—may each have a role in preparing for or responding to a communicable disease incident. That is, the specific response actions taken by individual entities, such as airports and airlines—as well as federal, state, and local authorities—will depend on the operating characteristics of the airline or airport, disease characteristics, and the type and level of threat that exists. Finally, some roles and responsibilities for a response to a threat in the aviation system are established in law or by agreement and others may be defined in preparedness plans. Airports are required by FAA regulations to develop airport-emergency plans (AEP), which must address a variety of hazards, including aircraft incidents and accidents, acts of terrorism, fires, natural disasters, hazardous materials, power failures, or water rescues.[22] These plans are not required to address communicable disease threats.

The risk of disease transmission in an airport and aboard airlines may be heightened during a communicable disease epidemic, although airports, airlines, and public health authorities may have to address travelers with more common communicable diseases such as tuberculosis or measles at any time. The recent Ebola epidemic in West Africa provides an example of a regional epidemic that triggered governments and aviation stakeholders to take additional precautions during each stage of air travel to minimize the spread of the disease. Figure 2 shows routine and potential enhanced safety measures that may be taken before, during, and after flights by a variety of stakeholders.

	Before flight	During flight	After flight
Routine communicable disease incident response	• Airlines observe ill passengers for health threats to other passengers	• Airline crew isolate and assess ill passengers, to the extent possible	• Screening for signs and symptoms during routine interactions
Enhanced response to communicable disease outbreak	• Exit screening • Funnel passenger or flights to designated airports	• Airline crew collect travel history	• Entry screening • Establish ongoing monitoring
If passenger poses sufficient risk of communicable disease	• Delay travel	• Airline crew report passenger illness	• On-site assessment and transport • Screening, evaluation, treatment, or transport • Restrict further travel • Federal, state, or local isolation or quarantine

Source: GAO. | GAO-16-127.

Figure 2. Potential Response by Flight Stage for Addressing Communicable Disease Threats from Abroad.

Before boarding an aircraft, passengers may be prevented from travel if they have a communicable disease that could pose a public health threat during the flight. For example, in the United States, DHS and HHS can identify travelers who are not allowed travel, based on public health threats.[23] Airlines may only refuse to board a passenger—or otherwise restrict or delay travel—with a communicable disease under DOT regulations if that passenger poses a direct threat to the health and safety of others.[24] Additionally, the Department of State can restrict visas for foreign travelers with a communicable disease, preventing them from entering the United States. Governments in areas experiencing such an outbreak may screen passengers exiting the area and restrict or discourage the transport of ill or possibly contagious passengers.

Under the IHR, these decisions may be made based on recommendations from WHO, although states can make their own entry- and exit-screening decisions. During the SARS epidemic, WHO recommended screening travelers before their departure from affected areas on international flights for symptoms associated with SARS and advising travelers with symptoms to postpone travel. To date, WHO has not recommended screening passengers departing from a U.S. airport, and the United States has never instituted such a precaution, according to CDC officials. Aviation stakeholders have questioned the legal authority by which the United States could implement exit screening. According to CDC officials, such screening could be done under HHS's quarantine and isolation authorities.[25]

CDC regulations require pilots to immediately report to CDC any deaths or the occurrence of any travelers with signs or symptoms that may indicate a communicable disease infection during international flights coming to the United States.[26] In the case of an ill traveler, CDC guidance recommends that the aircraft's crew take practical measures to protect themselves and others. These measures may include avoiding direct contact with bodily fluids, and if indicated, isolating ill passengers who exhibit specific signs or symptoms consistent with a communicable disease, as well as providing ill passengers with tissues or a mask. In conducting its assessment, CDC may also request that aircraft crewmembers hand out information about health risks or collect and report information on a suspected ill passenger's travel history, as done during the recent Ebola epidemic in West Africa. According to CDC officials, reporting suspected ill travelers before the flight's arrival gives ground-based responders preparation time to provide for medical assessment and treatment of the traveler upon arrival, if warranted.

Once an aircraft with a suspected ill passenger approaches an airport, decisions about where to park the aircraft, how to respond to the suspected ill passenger, and how to deplane other passengers may be coordinated among stakeholders, according to ICAO guidance. Federal or local public health officials, first responders (e.g., fire or emergency medical technicians), airport authorities, air traffic control personnel, or a combination of these stakeholders may make these decisions and lead certain components of the response based on the situation and available response protocols or preparedness plans. If a communicable disease is confirmed, CDC is to follow established protocols and work with state and local public health authorities to assess and provide interventions to other travelers onboard the aircraft, if necessary.

Passengers infected with respiratory, gastrointestinal, or blood-borne communicable diseases may contaminate aircraft or airports with bodily fluids.

Whether any measures beyond routine airline- and airport-cleaning practices are necessary will depend upon the characteristics of the disease in question, according to CDC guidance. For international flights, CDC may require additional cleaning or disinfection to prevent the transmission of a communicable disease.[27] Airline representatives told us that they may also opt for a more thorough decontamination as a precaution. Decontamination may be carried out by airport or airline staff or by contracted aviation-services firms.[28] During flights, cabin crew may clean potentially infectious material to protect other passengers, and CDC provides guidance on how to carry out this targeted cleaning. The occupational health and safety of airline, airport, or contracted aviation-service employees on the ground is overseen by OSHA, which sets and enforces workers' health and safety standards related to communicable diseases and provides guidance on personal protective equipment, decontamination, and handling waste contaminated by potentially infectious material, with certain exceptions.[29] On board an aircraft in operation, responsibility for the health and safety of employees is divided between the FAA and OSHA. FAA is responsible for all working conditions of flight crew (i.e., pilots, flight engineers, and flight navigators) and for most, but not all, working conditions of cabin crew (e.g., flight attendants).[30]

According to DOT's origin-and-destination ticketing data, almost 52-million air passengers entered the United States from other countries in 2014, including returning U.S. citizens. While the United States does not receive non-stop commercial flights from all countries, including the West African countries that suffered the recent Ebola outbreak, passengers come from every corner of the globe and fly into airports both large and small. Figure 3 shows passenger arrivals from five regions of the world and the top five airports receiving passengers whose travel originated from each of these regions in 2014 (for a total of 12 airports), based on the original departure airport in the ticket itinerary. Together, these 12 airports received about 50 percent of the total number of passengers coming into the United States from abroad in 2014—accounting for more than 25 million passenger arrivals.

Even if an ill passenger on an international flight is not detected while onboard an aircraft, he or she may be identified after arrival during the customs and immigration inspection process. After an international flight arrives in the United States, passengers are to undergo routine inspection or possibly enhanced screening for communicable diseases under authorities held by HHS[31] and DHS (by agreement).[32] During primary inspection, CBP staff are expected to visually observe arriving international travelers for certain signs and symptoms of communicable diseases during their routine interactions with travelers and then notify CDC, as appropriate.[33] CBP and CDC may investigate further by asking specific questions during primary inspection—such as inquiring about travel to affected areas—or by conducting additional assessments such as taking body temperatures during secondary or tertiary screening.

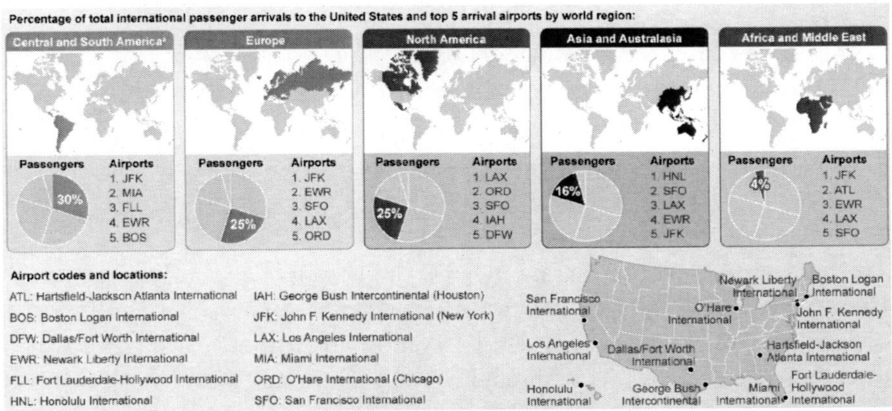

Sources: GAO analysis of Department of Transportation data and Map Resources. | GAO-16-127.

[a]Central and South America region includes the Caribbean.

Figure 3. Top Five U.S. International Arrival Airports for Five Global Regions, 2014.

For passengers who are asymptomatic (not displaying symptoms) but at heightened risk for a communicable disease, CDC officials may also establish a means of ongoing monitoring.[34] For example, asymptomatic passengers from Ebola-affected countries—Guinea, Liberia, and Sierra Leone[35]—receive a Check and Report Ebola (CARE) kit upon arriving in the United States if they are found to be at heightened risk of exposure. The kit contains guidance and tools to measure and report symptoms to local public health officials for the 21-day disease incubation period. Local public health authorities are responsible for protecting public health within their jurisdictions.[36] While CDC and state and local public health agencies coordinate closely on many issues, state and local public health authorities may, at their discretion and based on their legal authority, impose restrictions or requirements in their jurisdictions that are more stringent than those issued by CDC.[37]

In certain extraordinary circumstances, passengers or flights from areas experiencing a communicable disease outbreak could be redirected to designated U.S. airports with the capacity to receive them. This process is commonly referred to as "funneling," and it may involve re-routing passengers by changing their itineraries or directing flights to certain airports. Beginning in October 2014, for example, CBP directed all flights to the United States with passengers whose recent travel included Ebolaaffected countries to be routed to one of the following five designated airports where CBP and CDC staff conducted enhanced entry screening procedures:[38]

- John F. Kennedy International Airport,
- Newark Liberty International Airport,
- Washington Dulles International Airport,
- Hartsfield-Jackson Atlanta International Airport, and
- Chicago O'Hare International Airport

Prior to passenger re-routing by airlines, these five airports accounted for 94 percent of existing arrivals from the affected countries in West Africa (Guinea, Liberia, and Sierra Leone), according to CBP officials, all of which arrived on connecting flights through other countries.[39] Travelers who might have arrived at a different airport are now re-routed by airlines—or "funneled"—to arrive at one of these five designated airports. Any non-military U.S. health personnel returning from the Ebola-affected countries also have to return via these airports and go through enhanced screening.

Airports that are not designated to receive passengers from areas affected by a communicable disease outbreak may still encounter individuals who have recently traveled from affected areas even when funneling has been put in place. There have been Ebola-related responses at airports that were not identified for funneling, for example. One way this could happen is by a passenger traveling on a "broken ticket"—a separate itinerary for travel between the affected country and the United States via an intermediate destination, such as a country in Europe. In this instance, a passenger from an affected country may have bought two tickets—one to Europe and a separate ticket to the United States, following a layover. Another scenario is that a passenger could have transferred to a domestic flight after passing through a designated airport and developed symptoms of infection on the later flight. In cases such as these, CDC officials or local public health authorities, or both, may conduct public health assessments and follow-up activities.

AIRPORTS AND AIRLINES THAT WE REVIEWED HAVE PLANS, BUT A COMPREHENSIVE NATIONAL AVIATION-PREPAREDNESS PLAN DOES NOT EXIST

Airports and Airlines That We Reviewed Generally Have Communicable-Disease Preparedness Plans

Airports and Airlines We Reviewed Have Preparedness Plans

All of the 14 airports and three airlines we reviewed have plans—often contained in multiple documents—in place for responding to communicable disease threats from abroad. The plans in place for each airport and airline generally address the high-level components that we identified as common among applicable federal and international guidance.[40] We identified these components to provide a basis for assessing the breadth of the plans, not to evaluate the sufficiency of the plan's contents or the level of preparedness that the plans provide.

We found the plans in place at each of the 14 airports addressed the following six high-level components:

1. Establishment of an incident command center.
2. Coordination among various stakeholders.
3. Selection and use of personal protective equipment for various stakeholders.
4. Training for various stakeholders.
5. Some protocols for responding to a threat, such as meeting the aircraft, maintaining a quarantine area, or transporting a suspected ill passenger.
6. Protocols for decontamination.

The plans in place at each airport were developed by, or in collaboration with relevant airport stakeholders, including airport operators, first responders, state and local public health representatives, and officials from CDC and CBP, as applicable. Not all airports had a separate communicable-disease preparedness plan that alone addressed all six high-level components. For example, when asked about communicable-disease preparedness planning, representatives from 11 of the 14 airports reported that the procedures for responding to these threats at their airport were contained in multiple documents,[41] ranging from a general emergency preparedness plan, such as the airport-emergency plan (AEP)—required by FAA regulations, but not required to specifically address communicable diseases[42]—to a disease-specific preparedness plan, such as a pandemic influenza response plan. Other types of documents included a checklist for first responders; standard-operating procedures for a specific disease, such as Ebola; and CDC's communicable-disease response plans (which are discussed more below). During the Ebola outbreak, representatives from eight airports that we reviewed reported developing an additional Ebola-specific response plan or adapting an existing plan.

All three of the airlines we reviewed have a preparedness plan for responding to communicable disease threats. The plans themselves were not available to us because of their proprietary nature; however, based on our conversations with airline representatives and a review of summary information regarding their plans, we can report that the three airlines' plans addressed the following four high-level components:

1. Establishment of emergency response team and designation of emergency response center.
2. Description of the triggers that inform the level and nature of a response.
3. Activation triggers for the response team and response center.
4. Identification of roles and responsibilities for relevant stakeholders.

Furthermore, all three airlines stated that they carry universal precaution kits that include equipment to respond to suspected communicable diseases onboard aircraft flying internationally.[43]

As noted above, some airports have in place a CDC communicable-disease response plan (CDRP)—specifically 18 total airports that currently have (or had) a CDC quarantine station on site, 11 of which were included in our review. CDRPs fulfill part of WHO's IHR obligations for establishing core capacity at designated points of entry.[44] The CDRPs, according to CDC officials, were developed in coordination with relevant stakeholders and partners at each airport and based on a framework provided by CDC to airport quarantine stations. The existence of a CDRP at an airport does not preclude an airport operator or other airport stakeholders from developing and maintaining one or more additional preparedness plans or documents. In fact, representatives from all but one of the airports that we reviewed that have a CDRP reported having additional preparedness documents (10 of 11 airports). Representatives from 3 of those 10 airports that reported having plans contained in multiple documents do not view the CDRP as the airport's main preparedness plan for communicable diseases. One CDC official from the Quarantine and Border Health Services Branch noted that CDRPs at some airports are more developed than others and recognized that CDC quarantine staff in collaboration with relevant airport stakeholders are continually updating and improving the CDRPs. Figure 4 shows the 16 U.S. airports that currently have a CDC quarantine station and the 2 airports that formerly had one.[45] Each of these quarantine stations is also responsible for enforcing quarantine regulations at all airports within its assigned jurisdiction.

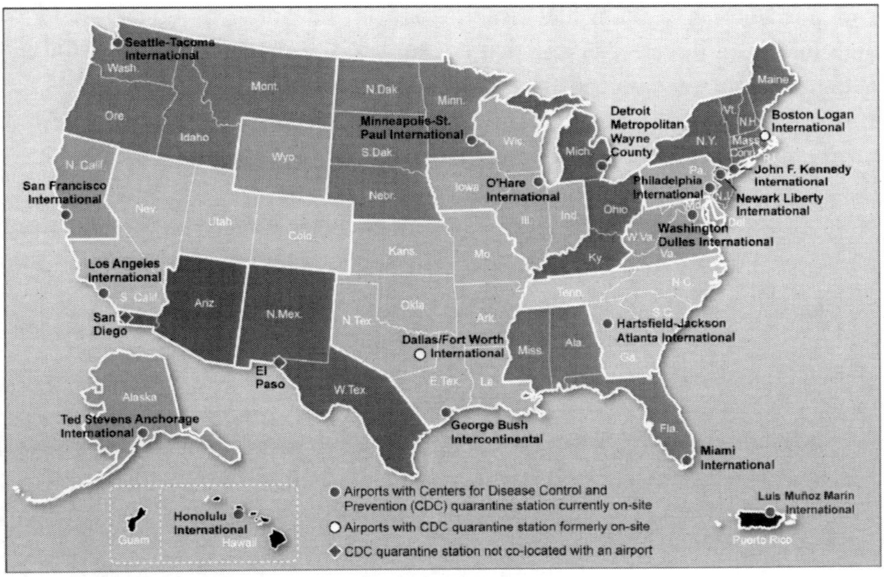

Sources: CDC and Map Resources. | GAO-16-127.

Figure 4. U.S. Airports with Centers for Disease Control and Prevention Quarantine Stations, 2015.

DOT officials told us that in 2010, DOT and the aviation industry requested that CDC expand its outreach to further the development of CDRPs beyond airports with quarantine stations on site to airports without them.[46] CDC officials told us that since that request, the agency has been working to expand the coverage of CDRPs to select U.S. airports. These officials told us that they are in the process of identifying priority airports using criteria that include the number and origins of arriving international passengers. These officials reported that at least three airports (one of which was included in our review) without quarantine stations on site have already collaborated with

CDC to develop an airport preparedness plan for communicable disease threats.[47] According to these officials, however, CDC response efforts to disease outbreaks, such as the cholera outbreak following the Haiti earthquake in 2010, have slowed these outreach efforts. CDC officials said they hope to complete this effort in the next several years, but do not have a specific established completion date.

FAA officials told us that they encourage airports and airlines to develop preparedness plans for communicable disease threats. For example, in July 2009, FAA Office of Airport Safety and Standards issued a CertAlert[48] to FAA airport inspectors to encourage airport operators to either update their pandemic flu plans—plans that airports may have developed in response to the avian influenza threat of H5N1 that began in 2003—or, for those that did not have a plan, to develop such a plan for their airport. In late 2014, FAA officials told us that they began planning an update of the July 2009 CertAlert, but it was delayed due to the Ebola response. As of August 2015, no updated CertAlert has been issued.

FAA officials told us that they do not track or review airport or airline plans—in part because they lack adequate public health expertise, which they believe CDC would have, to assess whether an airport's or airline's plan would be effective at preventing or reducing the spread of communicable diseases. FAA officials further noted that communicable diseases rarely threaten the safety of flight, which is FAA's primary regulatory jurisdiction. CDC officials in the Division of Global Migration and Quarantine office told us that they review CDRPs every 2 years at the 16 airports with quarantine stations currently on-site, and the CDC quarantine station staff at the airport review them during the in-between years. However, CDC officials noted that they do not formally track the development of any preparedness plans for communicable disease threats at airports that do not currently have a quarantine station on site.

Airports and airlines are not required to develop and maintain preparedness plans for communicable disease threats. And neither FAA nor CDC systematically tracks which airports and airlines have such plans. Thus, FAA and CDC officials could not tell us the full extent to which airports that receive international passengers and airlines that operate international flights have preparedness plans in place. The 18 airports with CDRPs accounted for about 58 percent of the international arriving passengers to the United States in 2014. These 18 airports— together with the 3 airports we reviewed without CDRPs, but with their own preparedness plans—accounted for about 65 percent of the international arriving passengers in 2014 (or about 34 million of the almost 52-million total).

A Variety of Entities Provide Resources to Help Develop Plans

A variety of entities, including FAA, CDC, state and local public health entities, and international sources, provide resources to help airports and airlines develop communicable-disease preparedness plans. In 2006, DOT, in coordination with CDC, published the *National Aviation Resource Manual for Quarantinable Diseases*,[49] which provides guidance for airports and airlines on how to develop a communicable-disease preparedness plan that can be adapted and implemented for a variety of sizes and types of communicable disease threats. When we asked representatives from three airports specifically about DOT guidance for preparedness plans during interviews, representatives from two airports were familiar with the Manual, but noted that it was outdated. An official from DOT's Office of Intelligence, Security, and Emergency Response told us that DOT has no plans to update it, in part, because in DOT's view, everything contained in the document can be found on other websites and doing so might create a document that could not be rapidly updated, as might be necessary in facing an emerging public health threat.

The guidance for specific disease threats that is published by CDC also provides some information for those attempting to develop plans or procedures for responding to a specific disease threat. For example, CDC published several guidance documents for airport and airline employees regarding Ebola, including guidance for personal protective equipment for airport and airline cleaning crews and interim guidance about Ebola infection for airline crews, cleaning personnel, and cargo personnel.[50] Local public health entities also provide resources, such as public health advisories, that airports reported using to help develop such plans.

Finally, some international guidance and technical assistance is available to airports and airlines in developing communicable disease plans.[51] For example, in 2009, ACI, in collaboration with ICAO, published the *Airport Preparedness Guidelines for Outbreaks of Communicable Disease* to help airports.[52] Through CAPSCA, ICAO works to bring international, regional, national, and local organizations together to combine efforts and develop a coordinated approach to respond to public health risks. CAPSCA's efforts include providing voluntary visits to airports to help them prepare for communicable disease threats.

The United States Lacks a Comprehensive National Aviation-Preparedness Plan

ICAO Standard Obligates Member States to Establish a National Aviation-Preparedness Plan

In 2007, ICAO adopted a standard that obligates each ICAO member state to establish a national aviation-preparedness plan for communicable disease outbreaks that pose a public health risk or public health emergency of international concern.[53] In 2010, ICAO, by resolution,[54] further urged member states to ensure that the public health sector and the aviation sector collaborate to develop a national preparedness plan for aviation to help prevent the spread of communicable diseases through air travel, and that member states establish requirements for the involvement of stakeholders, such as airport operators and airlines, in the development of the plan. In guidance to member states for developing a national aviation-preparedness plan, ICAO recommends that such a plan include guidance that is generic to all communicable diseases. This guidance can then be adapted for specific diseases. Officials from the DOT office responsible for coordinating U.S. policy for presentation to ICAO told us that it is the responsibility of each member state to either implement regulations or other appropriate measures to comply with ICAO standards or to file a "difference" with ICAO.[55]

While the United States has not developed a national aviation-preparedness plan for communicable disease outbreaks, DOT and CDC officials contend that some elements of such a plan already exist. Specifically, officials from DOT's Office of Intelligence, Security, and Emergency Response and FAA's Office of National Security Programs and Incident Response, as well as CDC's Division of Global Migration and Quarantine, told us that some elements of a national aviation-preparedness plan are encompassed in various documents that include airports' individual plans, including CDRPs at airports with quarantine stations on site. However, FAA reported to ICAO in 2010—by way of answering an ICAO questionnaire on member states' fulfillment of this standard[56]—that individual airport plans are intended to handle one or two flights with inbound passengers and not respond to a full epidemic, which may require a response involving multiple airports on a national level. Officials from CDC's Division of Global Migration and Quarantine also told us that while the United States does not have a national aviation-preparedness plan, past planning efforts, such as the 2005 *National Strategy for Pandemic Influenza* and its associated 2006 implementation plan developed in response to the avian influenza threat of H5N1,[57] as well as

CDC's Risk-Based Border Strategy (RBBS),[58] helped inform their decision making in the national-level response to Ebola as this response pertained to the screening and risk assessment of passengers arriving from the affected countries. The pandemic influenza national strategy and implementation plan, however, are neither aviation-specific nor designed to address communicable disease outbreaks of various types (e.g., different diseases), as we have found in past work.[59] Furthermore, CDC officials told us that the RBBS has been superseded by CDRPs, which represent the most up-to-date preparedness efforts at U.S. airports.

DOT and CDC officials also told us that while a national aviation-preparedness plan could have value, they do not believe that their respective agencies should be the lead in the development of such a plan. DOT officials said that a national aviation-preparedness plan for communicable disease outbreaks would be valuable to support a unified approach where multiple entities, including DOT, have input into the plan's development and can then test and exercise the plan. These officials also noted that while DOT's Office of the Secretary serves as the liaison to ICAO for Annex 9 to the Chicago Convention, in which the relevant ICAO standard is contained, complying with an ICAO standard could be led by any number of other federal agencies. DOT officials believe that while DOT should be a key contributor to the development of a national aviation-preparedness plan, HHS should be the lead federal agency in developing such a plan, in part because DOT does not have sufficient public health expertise, which they believe HHS does. CDC officials noted that since communicable disease is just one of many threats to the commercial aviation sector, a broader, all-hazards national aviation plan that includes communicable disease as a component may be more prudent or warranted.[60] These officials also noted that a standalone plan may not be necessary, as they believe that the elements currently in place are sufficient, as reflected in the successful national Ebola response effort. Yet these officials also stated that they could see value in aspects of a national aviation-preparedness plan where stakeholders come together to discuss preparedness, resulting in a document that is collaborative and likely agreed upon by relevant parties. CDC officials told us that if a national aviation-preparedness plan were to be developed, DOT would be in the best position to lead the effort because FAA and DOT have stronger and deeper ties to the relevant stakeholders that would be involved in such a broad effort. While the DOT and CDC may not agree on which agency should lead the development of a national aviation-preparedness plan, DOT's Office of the Secretary is the liaison to ICAO for

Annex 9 to the Chicago Convention, in which the relevant ICAO standard is contained, and is responsible for overseeing the aviation sector.

A National Plan Aims to Provide an Adaptable and Scalable Framework

ICAO's guidance to member states in developing a national aviation-preparedness plan also recommends that such a plan contain guidance that is generic to all communicable diseases and can be adapted to specific diseases. It also recommends that specific measures adopted at individual airports correspond to defined communicable disease threat alert levels, such as WHO's pandemic alert phases or a national public-health authority's alert levels, to help ensure that procedures are scaled up and down as circumstances of the public health threat change. Adopting measures that correspond to different risk levels or types of diseases would provide individual airports with an adaptable and scalable framework with which to align their plans—without which airports could find it challenging to prepare for a national response effort. For example, representatives from four airports that were not designated to conduct enhanced-screening for Ebola reported developing their own Ebola-specific response plans during the Ebola outbreak—sometimes with and sometimes without input from federal stakeholders. The airports did this in part because they did not know what their responsibilities would be in the long run or to what extent they would need to have procedures in place in the event that a suspected ill passenger was traveling on a broken ticket.[61] An adaptable and scalable framework would subsequently improve harmonization of individual plans across airports and airlines— helping ensure that the individual plans work in accordance with one another for a national level response effort—and serve as the basis for training airport and airline staff and crew.[62] For example, representatives from one airport told us that, in their view, many airports had good efforts under way to respond to Ebola, but that the efforts were fragmented across airports leaving passengers and airlines to deal with differences in how travel is handled at each airport.

Public-Health and Aviation Sector Coordination Has Been Insufficient

ICAO guidance to member states for developing a national aviation-preparedness plan for communicable disease outbreaks states that implementation of any measures within a preparedness plan should be a well-coordinated multi-agency effort to avoid confusion, inconsistencies, and duplication of resources, as well as minimize inconvenience to travelers. DOT officials reported not being involved in or consulted on the decision to funnel passengers from Ebola-affected countries to five airports and implement enhanced entry-screening procedures. And while the officials believe that funneling passengers was a good decision in the case of the Ebola threat, they expressed concern about what might happen during future national-level communicable disease response efforts if decisions affecting aviation are made without their input. For example, in response to the avian influenza threat of H5N1 that began in 2003, national efforts included discussions on funneling all international passengers through 30 U.S. airports and screening all arriving passengers—an option provided under RBBS.

Representatives from three of the four airports that we spoke with about this issue, as well as ACI representatives, expressed concern that funneling all arriving international passengers to 30 airports and screening them was unrealistic due to the resource requirements it would impose on airports and delays that could ripple across the national airspace system. DOT officials further noted that from an air traffic control perspective, many major U.S. airports are already at or near full capacity and shifting a significant amount of air traffic to these airports could result in gridlock. CDC officials acknowledged that funneling passengers to 30 airports and screening them all was a worst-case scenario and pointed out that RBBS was designed to be flexible and scalable and to serve as an adaptable framework for entry-screening at airports, as the RBBS framework did for the Ebola outbreak. DOT officials highlighted that because the number of passengers coming from the Ebola-affected countries is quite small relative to the total number of international passengers entering the United States (less than 25,000 out of almost 52- million total passenger arrivals in 2014), the impact from re-routing passengers to five airports and the time and resources needed to conduct the enhanced screening did not result in an unreasonable impact on the national aviation system. This may not be the case if the communicable disease threat were to come from China, for example, or another region with large numbers of passengers or flights to the United States.[63]

DOT officials also reported that they did not always have the opportunity or were provided insufficient time to review or comment on CDC Ebola guidance or fact-sheets addressed to aviation stakeholders. For example, a DOT official told us that because similar information was often posted in multiple places and because documents that the officials had reviewed in the past got renamed, revised, and re-published, the DOT official had to continue to watch out for published CDC guidance that included recommendations for the aviation industry. The DOT official highlighted that CDC guidance did not always have the DOT issues portrayed correctly and that failure to adequately coordinate with DOT could have safety consequences in some circumstances.

For example, if a disinfectant that is used to clean suspected Ebola contamination is not compatible with the aircraft materials (e.g., aluminum) or is used in the wrong manner, such as using too concentrated a solution, the aircraft could be damaged, which could negatively affect its airworthiness. Officials from CDC's Division of Global Migration and Quarantine acknowledged that some CDC webpages about Ebola developed prior to the beginning of the Ebola outbreak in 2014 contained misinformation related to aircraft disinfectants, but noted that the information was promptly removed once officials became aware of the problem. These officials also told us they sought DOT's input in guidance relevant to aviation, but acknowledged that at times during the Ebola outbreak, things moved very quickly and webpages were reorganized to make information easier to find.

Airports, Airlines, and other Stakeholders Faced Challenges Responding to Communicable Disease Threats and Are Taking Some Actions as a Result

While aviation stakeholders we spoke with reported having plans that address communicable diseases, they also reported facing multiple challenges in responding to threats and taking actions to address these challenges. Aviation stakeholders that we spoke with reported challenges in responding to communicable disease threats including obtaining guidance, communicating, coordinating among responders, and assuring employees have appropriate training, equipment, and sanitary workplaces. To address these challenges, aviation stakeholders reported taking actions such as developing communication tools and strategies; reviewing, exercising, and improving response plans; and providing training, equipment, and cleaning supplies. A national aviation-preparedness plan could serve as the basis for testing communication mechanisms among responders to ensure those mechanisms are effective prior to addressing a communicable disease outbreak. It could also serve as the basis to ensure that airport and airline staff have received appropriate training and access to properly maintained equipment to reduce the risk of exposure to communicable diseases during an outbreak.

Guidance and Communication Challenges

Stakeholders at 12 of the 14 airports we spoke with reported challenges in obtaining guidance on how to respond to communicable disease threats or in communicating during specific incidents. Various stakeholders including federal agencies, airports, airlines, and contracted aviation-services employers reported taking actions to improve access to timely guidance and communication. As we have found in prior work, planning efforts and exercises can help develop relationships between federal officials and stakeholders that are useful in responding to communicable diseases.[64] Moreover, ICAO recommends that national aviation-preparedness plans include a communication system and emphasizes the importance of periodically testing this communication system.

Guidance from Federal Agencies

Representatives at 7 of the 14 airports we spoke with reported difficulties obtaining prompt and clear guidance from federal agencies including CDC, CBP, and FAA on how to respond to specific communicable disease threats including Ebola. According to CDC, CDC Quarantine Station officials referred airport questions about the Ebola response to CDC headquarters to ensure airports received consistent guidance that reflected the most up-to-date information. However, representatives at 3 of the 10 airports with Quarantine Stations with whom we spoke said that CDC headquarters did not provide requested guidance within short time frames. Representatives from two airports said the initial federal response to Ebola was not clear because it did not correspond to a national plan or unified approach with which the representatives were familiar. In addition, a representative at another airport reported experiencing confusion determining the magnitude of the threat that Ebola posed and what guidance to follow given that FAA did not address these issues.

CDC officials we spoke with described inherent challenges to providing prompt guidance on the recent Ebola threat, as well as actions the agency took to address airports' and airlines' information needs during the response. Communicable disease outbreaks are unpredictable by their very nature. CDC officials told us that information evolved during the Ebola response and that answers to particular questions were not always readily available. In these instances, CDC formulated responses with the assistance of leadership and subject-matter experts. According to officials, CDC dedicated additional resources to provide in-depth and timely Ebola guidance, and met with aviation industry partners both collectively and individually.

Communications during Flight

Airport-emergency responders at 6 of the 14 airports we interviewed told us that airlines sometimes do not provide them with information that is as complete, accurate, and immediate as they would like when a traveler becomes ill during a flight. CDC officials also told us that information provided by airlines or air traffic control to CDC was often incomplete or inaccurate. While CDC requires pilots on international flights to U.S. airports to immediately notify CDC of ill travelers suspected of having a communicable disease[65]—as determined by signs and symptoms—flight crews must focus on safely operating the aircraft during critical phases of a flight such as takeoffs and landings.[66] This situation may preclude immediate notification, according to CDC officials. Furthermore, CDC officials and some responders we spoke with said that ill travelers or their caregivers may be reluctant or unable to share information, cabin crew may lack expertise in assessing relevant medical conditions, and information may develop inaccuracies as it passes from passenger to flight attendant to pilot to various ground-based responders. CDC officials also stated that a lack of proper equipment (thermometer, for example) on the aircraft may limit flight crews from providing a rapid and detailed notification of illness. CDC makes available guidance and tools to report traveler death or disease that outline reporting requirements and requested information.[67] However, airport responders and CDC officials said that airlines do not use a common template to record or communicate this requested information. Inaccurate or untimely information can slow down an appropriate response (such as conducting assessments before travelers have exited the aircraft) or trigger precautions unnecessarily. For example, representatives at one airport described launching an Ebola response after being alerted by an airline of a suspected case, only to discover that the passenger was traveling from East Africa—rather than an Ebola-affected area in West Africa—and suffering from a fear of flying rather than a physical illness.

Airport, airline, and other stakeholders have taken actions to improve communication about ill travelers during flights including real-time consultations with emergency medicine consultants, evaluating telemedicine technologies, and dedicating a radio frequency for emergencies to enable communication during flight with ground-based medical responders. See appendix II for additional information about technologies used to respond to communicable disease threats. In addition, CDC officials said that they conduct follow-up investigations when they receive reports of suspected communicable disease incidents on flights that airlines did not report and that CDC addresses with airlines any deficiencies found.

Aviation stakeholders have developed various tools to improve their communication about and response to medical problems. For example, one U.S. airline uses a checklist form to guide flight attendants in collecting and sharing traveler information with emergency medicine professionals who are remotely located. Another example comes from the AIRSAN Project, a stakeholder network that addresses response at the European Union level to public health threats in air transport. The AIRSAN Project developed operational tools including a flow chart and questionnaires to help cabin crew with decision making and information gathering to assess public health risks, communicate with ground-based responders (including public health officials who use the same tools), apply public health measures during the flight, and minimize interference with international traffic.

Communication after Arrival

Representatives at two of the three airlines we spoke with said that CDC does not routinely notify airlines of the results of an ill passenger's screening or diagnostic tests unless a positive diagnosis confirms a communicable disease. Representatives from one airline stressed that it experienced challenges obtaining information about the status of ill passengers or passengers who were not ill during flight but screened positive for risk of Ebola after leaving the aircraft. Representatives from this airline said these challenges impact their operations as well as their relationships with employees and customers. CDC officials confirmed that CDC does not routinely notify airlines when CDC determines a passenger's condition is not of public health concern or before diagnosing passengers suspected of communicable diseases. However, CDC protocols call for notifying airlines when a positive diagnosis confirms a communicable disease of public health concern. CDC officials also said that if there were suspicions but no diagnosis of a communicable disease, CDC might provide airlines with general information when media coverage or other concerns arise but would not provide personally identifiable information.[68]

All of the employees we spoke with from two contracted aviation-services firms that conduct aircraft cabin cleaning said that after incidents when a traveler became ill during a flight, the cabin crew does not always notify them of potentially infectious bodily fluids that had contaminated the aircraft. In its general infection-control guidance to airlines, CDC recommends that cabin crews notify cleaning crews of where and how ill passengers may have contaminated the aircraft and remind cleaning crews that additional personal protective equipment may be required. Given that it is typically unclear whether or not an illness that develops during a flight is contagious, CDC recommends treating any bodily fluid as potentially infectious regardless of whether or not an identified communicable disease outbreak threatens to spread to the United States. Aircraft cleaners we spoke with said that cleaning crews often have limited time to clean an aircraft before the boarding process begins for the next flight, and so may need to request additional time to conduct additional cleaning necessary to decontaminate the aircraft.

Some of the airlines and the contracted aircraft-cleaning employers we spoke with reported taking steps to improve communication about travelers' health status after leaving the aircraft and any contamination that cleaners may need to address. For example, a foreign airline has developed a paper-based form for cabin crews and public health officials to record and share information about potentially contaminated items on the aircraft and the disinfection agents the cleaning contractor should use. The contracted aircraft-cleaning employer we spoke with reported directing employees who clean international flights at one of the five enhanced screening airports for Ebola to notify their crew lead of any bodily fluids they encounter and to treat these fluids as potentially infectious.

Challenges in Providing Information to the Public

Keeping the traveling public informed about communicable disease risks and implications can help manage public anxiety to avoid unnecessary social disruption and economic losses, according to the WHO. WHO notes that intense public scrutiny may accompany a communicable disease incident, and DOT recommends in its *National Aviation Resource Manual for Quarantinable Diseases* that airports plan "how they will handle the onslaught of media inquiries and reports from the very outset of the communicable disease incident."

We interviewed airport representatives and their partners, such as emergency-management and public-health officials, and found that the need to provide public information in the wake of the Ebola outbreak and related airport incidents could create a variety of challenges. The 14 airports we spoke with and their partners provided the following xamples:

- Responding quickly enough to rapidly developing public concern: Some airport representatives said that suspected communicable disease incidents could quickly generate public concern. Representatives at three airports we spoke with emphasized the need to provide information quickly, and representatives at two of these airports stated a preference for a proactive rather than reactive approach to the media.
- Providing partners useful information: Emergency management officials at one airport conducting enhanced screening for Ebola and state public health officials working with this airport said they did not receive information needed to respond to media requests or inform senior public officials. However, representatives at another airport that conducts enhanced screening for Ebola noted that sharing information about a suspected communicable disease incident too broadly could cause unnecessary alarm.
- Addressing the volume of concerns: Representative from two airports said that addressing public information requests could require significant resources or create a challenging work environment.

Some airport representatives and union representatives also identified instances when information was requested that they believe should not be made available or could be better secured. For example, union representatives for cabin crews expressed concern that co-workers can identify crewmembers on a flight with an ill passenger and subsequently avoid working with them or even make their identities public via social media. Union representatives suggested that airlines could do more to protect crewmembers' identities after a potential communicable disease incident, but an airline we spoke with said that crewmembers' identities could be discovered by a variety of means outside of the control of the airline, including direct observation.[69]

Airport and airline representatives we spoke with identified actions they took to provide information about the Ebola threat to better inform the public. For example, three airports we spoke with highlighted using social media to provide information or respond to concerns in real time. Representatives from one of these airports and one of the three airlines we spoke with noted that it was useful to disseminate public information developed by CDC because of its credibility.

Challenges in Coordinating Incident Response

Representatives at 8 of the 14 airports that we interviewed identified challenges coordinating various entities' roles and actions when conducting communicable disease responses or exercises. Representatives from the 14 airports we spoke with and their partners reported challenges with:

- Lines of authority and plan alignment: Representatives from four airports we interviewed reported challenges determining lines of authority, such as whether CDC or fire department officials lead emergency medical services, or aligning stakeholders' response plans, such as airlines' plans, with the airports' response plans.
- Unnecessary interference: Representatives from three airports we spoke with reported that the actions of one type of responder had negative implications for another responder or for airport operations and that these complications were avoidable. For example, during the response to a passenger suspected of Ebola, responders blocked off a road to provide themselves with space to put on personal protective equipment. However, in so doing they blocked all baggage-handling trucks' access to the baggage claim area, and in turn, the baggage-handling trucks blocked other responders' access to the aircraft.
- Coordinating with contracted aviation-services firms: Representatives at two airports said that after completing the questionnaire we provided them, they realized that they likely should do more to coordinate with contracted aviation-services firms that operate at the airport.

Airport representatives reported taking various approaches to improve their coordination during a response. Airport officials reported using strategies such as conducting meetings or training with aviation stakeholders to provide information and clarify lines of authority in responding to communicable diseases, using centralized notification and communication hubs, and coordinating response activities through emergency operations centers or unified command structures. In addition, airport representatives at 2 of the 14 airports we interviewed highlighted their practice of reviewing the response plans of each airline operating at the airport to understand airlines' approach and assist with any gaps that the airport might identify. Representatives from each of the 14 airports we spoke with used some level of exercises and debriefs to improve the efficiency and effectiveness of their response, including four airports that conducted full-scale exercises that address simulated communicable-diseases incidents. In addition, airports debriefed staff involved with actual incidents that involve communicable disease response to assess and improve their operational capability. However, neither DOT nor HHS requires airports to conduct communicable disease exercises and debriefs, and the communicable disease exercises conducted by airports, varied in comprehensiveness from table-top to full-scale exercises, according to airport officials with whom we spoke.

According to an aviation medicine expert at ICAO, collaboration between aviation and public health officials presents the biggest challenge in managing communicable diseases in the aviation sector. For example, under airport all-hazards plans, officials typically isolate aircraft away from the terminal in order to minimize suspected threats (e.g., bomb threats), but in a public health emergency it may be more appropriate to park an aircraft near the terminal to provide emergency responders access, according to this expert. Representatives from 3 of the 14 airports we interviewed mentioned adapting their practices during the Ebola outbreak or recent exercises to park incoming aircraft with ill travelers suspected of communicable diseases at or near the gate rather than at a remote location.

Challenges in Training and Equipping Contracted Aviation-Service Employees

Contracted aviation-service employees—including airport cleaning, aircraft cleaning, and passenger-service employees (e.g., wheelchair attendants), and associated union representatives we interviewed— expressed concern that these service employees did not receive adequate communicable disease training and reported challenges accessing appropriate personal protective equipment, cleaning equipment, and cleaning supplies. Inadequate training, equipment, and supplies could lead to employee exposures to pathogens that could in turn result in infections. This risk could extend to passengers since they share the same aircraft environment. OSHA violations provide some evidence for concerns and challenges related to appropriate pathogenexposure-control planning, training, vaccinations, and personal protective equipment.

OSHA's blood-borne pathogens standard requires employers to provide employees who encounter blood, certain bodily fluids, and other potentially infectious materials while carrying out job duties with:

- Training: initial and annual training—including the opportunity to ask questions of a knowledgeable trainer—on methods to control exposures to pathogens and additional training when changes occur that affect employees' occupational exposure to potentially infectious materials.[70]
- Personal protective equipment: appropriate personal protective equipment such as gloves, gowns, eye protection, and masks.[71]
- Sanitary work surfaces: work surfaces that have been noticeably contaminated by potentially infectious materials must be decontaminated with an appropriate disinfectant immediately or as soon as feasible.[72]
- Vaccination and post-exposure evaluation and follow-up: employees must be offered the hepatitis B vaccination and be evaluated and provided follow-up after an exposure incident.[73]

We spoke with nine workers employed by aviation-services firms that contract with airports or airlines. Collectively, these nine employees worked for four different firms at four separate airports. Employees and union representatives we spoke with reported gaps in training, equipment, supplies, and time to decontaminate aircraft.

- No routine or outbreak-specific training: Employees from three of the four contracted aviation-services firms that we spoke with said that employers do not provide formal, hands-on training to understand risks and minimize workers' exposure to potentially infectious materials, and that employers did not provide hand-on training to respond to specific disease outbreaks such as Ebola.[74] For example, aircraft cabin cleaners from one firm reported not knowing where to dispose of hazardous material and so sometimes simply disposed of it with non-hazardous garbage.
- Inadequate personal protective equipment: Aircraft cabin cleaners we spoke with from the two firms that conduct cabin cleaning reported that the gloves employers provided were too thin and that they could not replace gloves immediately if they ripped because of the need to clean aircraft quickly.[75]
- Unsanitary conditions and unavailable resources to clean: Wheelchair attendants at both airports where we interviewed passenger-service employees reported that wheelchairs were not always decontaminated

after coming in to contact with potentially infectious materials such as feces.[76] Employees with each of the three firms that conduct airport or aircraft cabin cleaning reported lacking sufficient and clean towels. For example, one employee said that cabin cleaners sometimes use the same towels to clean potentially infectious materials and later to clean food service equipment such as coffeemakers. Employees at two of the three firms that conduct cleaning reported difficulties accessing cleaning solutions, and employees we interviewed from one of the two firms that conduct aircraft cabin cleaning said that cleaning solutions sometimes are not properly labeled, causing them to use the wrong concentration.

- Insufficient time to clean: A union representative and employees we interviewed from one of the two firms that conduct aircraft cabin cleaning noted that some cleaning solution instructions indicate that the solution should sit for a period of time on potentially contaminated surfaces before cleaning, but that this was not always possible when cleaners have to quickly prepare the aircraft for another flight.

Violations of state and federal occupational health standards by contracted aviation-services employers provide some support to employees' concerns that aviation services' employers do not always ensure that their employees received blood-borne pathogen training and personal protective equipment. Union representatives provided us with examples of citations between December 2012 and July 2015 resulting from complaints aviation-service employees filed with the union's assistance. We used publicly available information from OSHA to confirm that at least 11 of these citations resulted in violations of OSHA's blood-borne pathogens standard or analogous state standards that are at least as effective.[77] Among these violations were instances when aviation-services employers did not provide employees with appropriate pathogen exposure control planning, training, vaccinations, and personal protective equipment. Eight of the 11 violations were designated serious violations, which indicates a substantial probability that death or serious physical harm could result, unless the employer did not, and could not with the exercise of reasonable diligence, know of the presence of the violation. In total, OSHA found that these 11 violations led to 680 instances when conditions did not meet OSHA's blood-borne pathogens standard, and almost all of these instances (676 out of 680) affected over 100 employees. OSHA records indicate that employers took corrective actions to address these violations.

We interviewed representatives from two aviation-services employers that contract with airports and airlines, and both said that they comply with training, personal protective equipment, and decontamination standards required by regulation. Representatives from the firm that conducts aircraft cabin cleaning said that airlines provide employees with labeled cleaning products that trained managers dilute to ensure that the products used are appropriate as indicated by the original-equipment manufacturer. In addition to providing employees with required training, personal protective equipment, and supplies, representatives from both aviation-services firms that we spoke with reported taking additional precautions during the Ebola outbreak such as providing employees with additional hands-on training, personal bottles of hand sanitizer, and information about Ebola on tablet devices that some employees use to carry out job duties.

In addition, airports, airlines, and union representatives we spoke with reported taking steps to mitigate aviation-service employees' exposure to communicable diseases, especially since the Ebola threat emerged. For example, representatives from two airports we spoke with have established airport minimum standards—including hazardous material training—to qualify or license aviation-services firms that operate at the airport. Representatives from all three airlines we spoke with said that they provided contracted firms with additional information to help them prepare for the Ebola threat and reported taking steps to ensure that contracted employers provide employees appropriate training and personal protective equipment. Union representatives also reported providing training on infection control for aviation-service employees at some international airports during the Ebola outbreak.

CONCLUSION

Air travel—more than any other mode of transportation—creates the potential for infected persons to move quickly from one part of the world to another while sharing confined quarters with other travelers. With the anticipated growth in international air travel, the recurring threat of communicable diseases from abroad, and the potential economic cost of disrupting air travel, it is imperative that the U.S. aviation system is sufficiently prepared to help respond to any communicable disease threat. The 14 airports that we reviewed (11 of which have CDC-developed CDRPs) had a plan or plans in place that in combination with one another met the six high-level components that we identified as common components in federal and international guidance. CDC is working to expand development of CDRPs to select U.S. airports that the agency is currently identifying, using criteria involving the origins and the total volume of international arriving passengers, but it is uncertain when CDC will be able to complete this effort. Furthermore, Annex 9 to the Chicago Convention obligates member states to establish a national aviation-preparedness plan—a plan intended to provide a mechanism for the public health sector to coordinate with the aviation sector in the event of a communicable disease threat. Yet DOT and CDC officials acknowledge that only certain "elements" of a national aviation-preparedness plan are in place. Such a plan could help maximize an effective response to a public health threat, while minimizing potential inefficiencies in the national response effort and unnecessary disruptions to the national aviation system. A national aviation-preparedness plan that is generic to all communicable diseases and can be adapted for specific diseases would provide individual airports and airlines with an adaptable and scalable framework with which to integrate their individual plans and promote harmonization of individual plans across airports and airlines. As such, the plan could also serve as the basis for testing communication mechanisms among responders to help ensure those mechanisms are effective. In addition, it could help ensure that airport and airline staff have received appropriate training and access to properly maintained equipment during an outbreak to reduce the risk of exposure to communicable diseases. Finally, DOT officials expressed concern about their lack of involvement in decisions made during the Ebola outbreak that involved the aviation sector. Developing and maintaining a national aviation-preparedness plan could foster a shared understanding and agreement among all relevant stakeholders, and help balance the needs of the aviation and public health sectors.

RECOMMENDATION

To help improve the U.S. aviation sector's preparedness for future communicable disease threats from abroad, we recommend that the Secretary of Transportation work with relevant stakeholders, such as the Department of Health and Human Services, to develop a national aviation-preparedness plan for communicable disease outbreaks. Such a plan could establish a mechanism for coordination between the aviation and public health sectors and provides clear and transparent planning assumptions for a variety of types and levels of communicable disease threats.

Agency Comments and Our Evaluation

We provided a draft of this product to DOT, HHS, DHS, Labor, and State for comment. DOT partially concurred with our recommendation. State did not provide comments to include in this report. HHS, DHS, and Labor only provided technical comments that we incorporated, as appropriate.

With regard to our recommendation, DOT agreed that there is a need for a national aviation-preparedness plan for communicable diseases to help improve the U.S. aviation sector's preparedness for future communicable disease threats. DOT further proposed that those agencies that have both legal authority and expertise for public health take the lead role in developing such a plan within the existing interagency framework for national-level all-hazards emergency preparedness planning, for which DOT stands ready to participate. We agree that public health expertise is needed in developing a national aviation-preparedness plan. However, as stated in our report, DOT has primary responsibility in overseeing the aviation sector and DOT's Office of the Secretary is the liaison to ICAO for the Annex to the Chicago Convention that obligates member states to establish a national aviation-preparedness plan. As such, we believe that DOT is in the best position to work with its relevant stakeholders, including those that have the needed public health expertise, to develop a national aviation-preparedness plan. DOT also provided technical comments that we incorporated, as appropriate.

Sincerely yours,
Gerald L. Dillingham, Ph.D. Director
Physical Infrastructure Issues

Appendix I: Objectives, Scope, and Methodology

Objectives

GAO was asked to review the preparedness of the U.S. aviation system in responding to communicable disease threats from abroad. This report examines:

1. The extent to which selected U.S. airports and airlines have preparedness plans to respond to communicable disease threats from

abroad and the extent to which a national aviation-preparedness plan guides preparedness.

2. Challenges that U.S. airports and airlines including contractors have faced when responding to threats and the actions have they taken to help address those challenges.

Scope

Characteristics of communicable disease threats from abroad: We considered the following characteristics as applicable to the scope of our review:

- communicable disease of public significance (e.g., non-routine diseases, including Ebola, SARS, and MERS),
- international arriving traveler,
- suspected ill traveler is identified onboard an arriving aircraft, or
- suspected ill traveler is identified in an airport after deplaning aircraft.

We considered the following characteristics as not applicable to the scope of our review:

- traveler who is ill with seasonal flu or other routine disease that is not of public significance,
- solely domestic travelers,
- threat of communicable disease spread by cargo or animals,
- bioterrorism (i.e., traveler using communicable disease as a weapon),
- continuity of Operations, and
- known medical transport (ill person is identified prior to departing host country).

Selected airports and airlines: We selected for review 14 airports—which accounted for about 53 percent of total international arriving passengers in 2014—that met one or more of the following criteria (see table 1):

- have enhanced passenger entry-screening procedures in place for international passengers arriving from the three current or past Ebola-affected countries in West Africa;

- received the first and second largest number of international passengers from each of five world regions in 2014;
- large hub airports[1] with a Centers for Disease Control and Prevention (CDC) quarantine station on site at the time of our review;
- large hub airports without a CDC quarantine on site, but still receiving a larger number of international passengers relative to other large hubs without a CDC quarantine station on site;
- experienced a confirmed Ebola case;
- have a station manager from one of the three U.S. airlines in our review; and
- are located within proximity to a GAO office.

Table 1. Selected Airports for Review

Airport	Centers for Disease Control and Prevention (CDC) quarantine station on site	Ebola enhanced entry screening	First and second highest number of international passenger arrivals from one or more world regions in 2014
Dallas/Fort Worth International	[a]		
Fort Lauderdale-Hollywood International	[b]		
Hartsfield-Jackson Atlanta International	X	X	X
Honolulu International	X		X
John F. Kennedy International	X	X	X
Los Angeles International	X		X
McCarren International (Las Vegas)	[b]		
Miami International	X		X
Newark Liberty International	X	X	X
O'Hare International (Chicago)	X	X	X
Orlando International	[b]		
Seattle-Tacoma International	X		
San Francisco International	X		X
Washington Dulles International	X	X	

Source: CDC and GAO analysis of DOT's O&D data.

[a]Dallas Fort-Worth formerly had a CDC quarantine station on site.

[b]Large hub airports without a CDC quarantine on site, but still receiving a larger number of international passengers relative to other large hub airports without a CDC quarantine station on-site.

We selected for review the three U.S. airlines that handle the largest quantity of international passengers—American Airlines, Delta Air Lines, and United Airlines.

Departments and components: Our review involved five federal departments—the Departments of Transportation (DOT), Health and Human Services (HHS), Homeland Security (DHS), State, and Labor. We selected these departments because they represent the key federal departments with responsibilities for preparing for and responding to communicable disease threats from abroad. Within these five departments we collected and reviewed available documentation and interviewed officials from various components that play a key role at their respective departments for these matters, principally DOT's Federal Aviation Administration (FAA), HHS's CDC, DHS's U.S. Customs and Border Protection (CBP), and Labor's Occupational Safety and Health Administration (OSHA).

Methodology

To examine the extent to which airports and airlines have plans in place to respond to communicable disease threats from abroad, we developed and administered a questionnaire to airport operators of the 14 selected airports on general preparedness at their airport.[2] The questionnaire included questions about communication with local stakeholders about communicable diseases, guidance used to develop any plans for communicable disease response, and plans or procedures that the airport had in place for a variety of situations or stakeholders, such as establishing the parking location for an aircraft and training for airport employees. We then conducted follow-on interviews with the 14 airport operators and relevant local stakeholders, who generally included first responders, local public health officials, CBP officials, and CDC officials, if applicable, about their preparedness. We also collected from the 14 selected airports and 3 selected airlines relevant and available preparedness plans for communicable disease threats. We identified and reviewed applicable federal requirements and international obligations, including the International Civil Aviation Organization's (ICAO) Standards and Recommended Practices, and guidance for U.S. airports and airlines with international air traffic. We identified high-level components that were common across applicable federal and international guidance, obligations, and requirements, as well as corroborating information collected from aviation stakeholders with whom we spoke.[3] We then developed a list of high-level components for airports' and airlines' communicable-disease preparedness plans to provide a basis for assessing the breadth of the plans. We compared these high-level components against the available plans collected from the 14 airports and three airlines as a method to assess the breadth of the plans. We then reviewed the structure and contents of these plans, but did not evaluate the plans for sufficiency or level of preparedness. We reviewed available documents from the five selected federal departments and their relevant components and interviewed officials from these departments. We also interviewed representatives from federal and international airport, airline, and flight-attendant industry associations,[4] and ICAO about preparedness plans generally and potential opportunities to improve preparedness.

To examine challenges that U.S. airports and airlines, including contractors, have faced when responding to communicable disease threats, including Ebola, and the actions they have taken to help address those challenges, we first identified challenges through interviews with selected airports and airlines as discussed above, as well as interviews with representatives from the labor union representing airport- and airline-service employees, and airport- and airline-contract employers of service employees. We consulted with representatives from the union that represents these employees to identify nine aviation-service employees with whom we spoke, and we conducted interviews with two of the four firms that these nine employees worked for, as well as three of the four airports they worked at. We also identified challenges to responding to communicable disease threats and actions taken by stakeholders during our attendance at a Global Symposium—convened by ICAO in collaboration with the World Health Organization (WHO)—of the Collaborative Arrangement for the Prevention and Management of Public Health Events in Civil Aviation (CAPSCA) program, which is a global, collaborative arrangement that works to bring together international, regional, national, and local organizations to develop a coordinated approach to preparedness and response. We also collected and reviewed available after-action reports that airports used to assess their responses to simulated communicable disease incidents. In addition, to corroborate comments we heard from airline-service employees (e.g., aircraft cabin cleaners or wheelchair attendants) and their union representatives, we reviewed summaries of inspections and violations related to OSHA's blood-borne pathogens standard that were initiated by employees with the support of their union. The challenges faced by U.S. airports, airlines, and contracted aviation-services firms and the actions taken to address these challenges that we describe in this report represent information provided to us during interviews and site visits, but may not capture all of the challenges and actions taken by the airports, airlines, and aviation-services firms we spoke with.

We conducted this performance audit from November 2014 to December 2015 in accordance with generally accepted government auditing standards. Those standards require that we plan and perform the audit to obtain sufficient, appropriate evidence to provide a reasonable basis for our findings and conclusions based on our audit objectives. We believe that the evidence obtained provides a reasonable basis for our findings and conclusions based on our audit objectives.

APPENDIX II: TECHNOLOGIES FOR RESPONDING TO COMMUNICABLE DISEASES IN AVIATION

A few technologies have been implemented, or are being developed, to identify or mitigate potential outbreaks of communicable diseases through air travel. These include screening passengers to detect travelers who may have an infectious disease (ill travelers), utilizing temperature screening to diagnose ill travelers, and using data analysis to identify disease outbreaks and potential traveler movement patterns.[1]

Temperature-Screening Technologies

U.S. Customs and Border Protection (CBP) personnel routinely observe travelers during their primary inspection and refer those that show symptoms of a communicable disease—or those recently traveling from an area of concern—for further assessment by Centers for Disease Control and Prevention (CDC) staff or other health authorities. Additional screening, such as was carried out during the Ebola threat, may include more targeted assessments during enhanced screening. According to the CBP, there are three main screening methods used for identifying passengers entering the United States who may have communicable diseases during the Ebola outbreak: (1) collecting advance passenger information, (2) visual inspection or taking of temperatures, and (3) questioning travelers. All of these methods are used for screening airplane passengers arriving in the United States, but only temperature measurement is associated with on-site health technology. Temperature checks may be conducted with contact or noncontact thermometers, but outside of the current Ebola response, this check is typically not common and only done in the setting of assessment of a suspected ill traveler reported to CDC, according to CDC officials.

Entry screening for Ebola at enhanced screening airports in the U.S. includes using non-contact infrared thermometers, under the enhanced screening protocols put in place to address the disease threat. Non-contact thermometer-based temperature measurement is a simple enough premise, but an agency official suggested it has both low sensitivity and specificity for detecting passengers with infectious disease.[2] In other words, such temperature measurement alone has a low chance of correctly identifying ill travelers and a low chance of correctly excluding healthy travelers. In the case of enhanced screening for Ebola, CDC officials or CBP contractors use thermometers that are commercially available following primary inspection by CBP personnel. To date, no mass screening of airplane passengers—where every passenger's temperature is taken—has been conducted at a U.S. airport. During the recent Ebola outbreak, for example, only passengers with recent travel to, from, or through outbreak countries, such as Sierra Leone, were identified for temperature screening.

Internationally, both non-contact infrared thermometers as well as thermal scanners have been used for entry and exit passenger screening for communicable diseases, including Ebola and severe acute respiratory syndrome (SARS). For example, in 2009, during the H1N1 influenza pandemic, many international airports—but not U.S. airports— implemented temperature-screening procedures. However, the literature reports questionable effectiveness from temperature screening, stemming in part from the aforementioned low sensitivity.[3] Some of the performance issues result from variabilities in temperature measurements exceeding the threshold for fever indication—variabilities of up to 3 degrees Celsius under some circumstances, such as after smoking, whereas fever can be indicated by an elevation of 1 degree Celsius for Ebola, for example. Temperature variability results from several factors including metabolism, medication, environment, and conditions, such as certain cancers, which are not quarantinable diseases of concern for airport screening purposes. Further, passengers who are in the incubation period of illness may not exhibit fevers, given that such periods of several infectious diseases typically last longer than most flights. According to scientific literature, camera-based thermograms have been used internationally. For example, camera-based temperature measurement, followed by ear-based temperature measurement, has been tentatively shown to be effective for monitoring Dengue Fever in Taiwan. Dengue fever is not a

U.S. quarantinable disease, and another study indicated uncertainty that temperature screening is effective for mitigating community transmission of this disease. Generally, however, thermal cameras are more expensive than thermometers and their precision is not better. A possible reason for deploying thermal cameras is the eventual capacity to screen large numbers of travelers rapidly, but the benefits of this approach have not been established.

BioMosaic

The CDC has developed a "Big Data" approach for identifying and tracking communicable disease outbreaks through data collection and analysis.[4] Information provided by BioMosaic can be used to help determine the risk of international spread of disease and to target potential CDC intervention by identifying potential threats, although it cannot be used to identify specific ill individuals. Launched in 2011 by the CDC's Division of Global Migration and Quarantine, BioMosaic is a data analytics tool that works with collections of data, including news sources, historical travel information, and public databases to map the health and demographics of foreign-born populations within the United States (e.g., diaspora), as well as disease outbreaks internationally.[5]

For example, in 2014, the CDC reported the first confirmed cases of Middle East Respiratory Syndrome (MERS) infections in the United States and, by using BioMosaic, was able to identify the major points of entry into the country, as well as the volume of travelers entering from Saudi Arabia and the United Arab Emirates. CDC was able to identify five cities within the United States that accounted for 75 percent of arrivals from those two countries.

Flight-Related Medical Technologies

Several technologies are being evaluated for potential use in tracking or mitigating disease, including communicable diseases. These technologies could potentially be used for air travel. These include (1) telemedicine, (2) air circulation control, (3) genetic sequencing of airplane lavatory waste, and (4) point-of-care diagnostic technology. These technologies are at various stages of development and their effectiveness and cost considerations are not established.

Airlines use a variety of approaches in responding to ill passengers during flight. United Airlines is currently exploring the use of telemedicine, whereby some technology can be used on board an aircraft to provide a remotely located doctor with information—such as vital signs—needed for diagnosis and determining whether a flight diversion is needed.

Development of altered air circulation devices may also mitigate the spread of communicable diseases. Currently, air in an aircraft is filtered by high-efficiency particulate air (HEPA) filters, but effectiveness relies on the air's passing through the filters. If a pathogen circulates widely within an aircraft cabin prior to being filtered, there may be an increased chance of person-to-person transmission of the disease. Air-circulation-altering devices may provide more isolated air environments for each passenger, but these devices have not yet been developed to the point where they have been tested or validated.

Recent research used meta-genomic examination of the content of airplane lavatories by sequencing and detecting the relative abundance of select pathogens (not quarantinable infectious diseases, however). By isolating and determining the sequence from genetic material found in passenger bio-waste, the researchers were able to determine the types of antibiotic resistance carried by passengers' microbes. Researchers were also able to identify specific pathogens, as well as their relative abundance based on the geographic origin of the samples. This method is potentially useful for global surveillance of communicable diseases, antibiotic resistances, and transmission routes. However, there are potential challenges to implementing this approach. For example, the researchers identified that implementing this method from all flights on a weekly basis would be challenging, given the current state of technology.

Additionally, developments in point-of-care technology—methods that can be used in doctor's offices, hospitals, or on the field (e.g., at an airport), instead of a laboratory—are increasing the speed of diagnosis as well as the variety of diseases that can be targeted. For example, companies have developed FDA-approved tests for human immunodeficiency virus (HIV) that do not require laboratory equipment and can provide results in as little as 20 minutes. Some tests for communicable diseases, such as influenza, have been developed and FDA-approved, but studies have indicated the sensitivities can be variable. Future improvements may lead to feasible screening based on, for example, microfluidics devices that can identify multiple concomitant infections.

End Notes

[1] For more information about the interaction of the aviation sector and communicable disease threats, see Airport Cooperative Research Program, Transportation Research Board, *Interagency–Aviation Industry Collaboration on Planning for Pandemic Outbreaks*, Conference Proceedings 41 (Washington, D.C.: 2008).

[2] IATA, *Economic Briefing: Avian Flu* (May 2006).

[3] According to the Centers for Disease Control and Prevention (CDC), *epidemic* refers to an increase, often sudden in the number of cases of a disease above what is normally expected in that population in that area. *Outbreak* carries the same definition of epidemic, but is often used for a more limited geographic area. Finally, *pandemic* refers to an epidemic that has spread over several countries or continents, usually affecting a larger number of people.

[4] GAO, *Influenza Pandemic: Lessons from the H1N1 Pandemic Should Be Incorporated into Future Planning,* GAO-11-632 (Washington, D.C.: June 27, 2011).

[5] Airport Council International (ACI) and International Civil Aviation Organization (ICAO), *Airport Preparedness Guidelines for Outbreaks of Communicable Disease*, Revised (April 2009); IATA, *Emergency Response Plan: A Template for Air Carriers* (May 2009).

[6] U.S. commercial service airports accounting for 1 percent or more of total annual U.S. passenger enplanements. 49 U.S.C. § 47102(10).

[7] American Airlines, Delta Air Lines, and United Airlines.

[8] Airport Council International (ACI) North America, Airlines For America, and Association of Flight Attendants.

[9] We consulted with representatives from the union that represents these workers to identify aviation service employees to speak with, and we conducted interviews with two of the four firms that the nine employees identified worked for, as well as three of the four airports where they worked.

[10] WHO, *Outbreak Communication: Best Practices for Communicating with the Public during an Outbreak,* Report of the WHO Expert Consultation on Outbreak Communications held in Singapore, September 21–23, 2004.

[11] The revised IHR (2005) were adopted by the World Health Assembly on May 23, 2005, and became effective in the summer of 2007.

[12] ICAO is a United Nations specialized agency created in 1944 by the Convention on International Civil Aviation (Chicago Convention), under which ICAO Member States agreed, among other things, "to take effective measures to prevent the spread by means of air navigation of cholera, typhus (epidemic), smallpox, yellow fever, plague and such other communicable diseases as the [ICAO Member] States shall from time to time decide to designate." Art. 14, Chicago Convention.

[13] Article 19 of the IHR.

[14] The ICAO Standard contained in paragraph 8.12 of Annex 9 (Facilitation) to the Chicago Convention states that "[ICAO Member] States shall comply with the pertinent provisions of the IHR. Member states are not obligated to follow the recommended practices, although these may also be used to develop regulations or guidance by the relevant agency of the member state's government.

[15] Member states are obligated to notify ICAO of a "difference" from the international standard, if they find it impractical to fully comply with an international standard or otherwise differ from the standard in their regulations or practices. Art. 38, Chicago Convention.

[16] ICAO, *Template for a National Aviation Public Health Emergency Preparedness Plan*, accessed December 31, 2014, http://www.capsca.org/Documentation/TemplateAviation PHEPNov2010.pdf.

[17] CBP possesses broad authority under customs and immigration laws to examine merchandise, cargo, conveyances, and persons upon their entry to and exit from the United States. 19 U.S.C. §§ 482, 1461, 1496, 1499, 1581, 1582, 1589a, and 1595; 8 U.S.C. §§ 1222, 1225, and 1357.

[18] Under section 361 of the Public Health Service Act (codified at 42 U.S.C. § 264), HHS is authorized to make and enforce regulations to prevent the entry and spread of communicable diseases from foreign countries into the United States and among states. The authority for carrying out these functions on a daily basis has been delegated to CDC, an agency in HHS. Under 42 C.F.R. parts 70 and 71, CDC may provide for the detention, medical examination, and release of persons arriving into the United States and traveling among states who are suspected of carrying these communicable diseases. Quarantinable diseases include cholera, diphtheria, infectious tuberculosis, plague, smallpox, yellow fever, viral hemorrhagic fevers (including Ebola), severe acute respiratory syndromes, and flu that can cause a pandemic (Executive Order No. 13674, § 1, 79 Fed. Reg. 45671 (July 31, 2014)).

[19] Several OSHA standards and directives are directly applicable to protecting workers against transmission of infectious agents. These include OSHA's Bloodborne Pathogens standard (29 C.F.R. § 1910.1030), which provides protection of workers from exposures to blood and body fluids that may contain blood-borne infectious agents; OSHA's Personal Protective standard (29 C.F. R. § 1910.132) and Respiratory Protection standard (29 C.F. R. § 1910.134) which provide some protection for workers when exposed to infectious agents transmitted through routes other than the bloodborne route; and OSHA's TB compliance directive which protects workers to a certain degree against exposure to TB through enforcement of existing applicable OSHA standards and the General Duty Clause of the OSH Act (29 U.S.C. § 654).

[20] A visa does not guarantee entry into the United States.

[21] For purposes of this report, we refer to state, local, and tribal public health authorities as local public health authorities.

[22] 14 C.F.R. § 139.325. See also FAA, *Advisory Circular: Airport Emergency Plan,* 150/5200-31C (Washington, D.C.: July 19, 2009).

[23] When HHS requests DHS assistance, HHS notifies TSA of individuals it has identified as public health threats who should be designated "Do Not Board." The public health "Do Not Board" list—created in response to concerns about prior drug-resistant tuberculosis-traveler incidents—is designed to ensure that airlines are notified that they should not allow the designated individuals on any commercial flights to or from the United States. See GAO, *Public Health And Border Security: HHS and DHS Should Further Strengthen Their Ability to Respond to TB Incidents,* GAO-09-58 (Washington, D.C.: Oct. 14, 2008).

[24] An airline can refuse to transport a person with a communicable disease to the extent permitted by the airline's contract of carriage and DOT's disability regulation, 14 C.F.R. Part 382. Under DOT nondiscrimination regulations, passengers who have a communicable disease or infection may only be prevented from traveling; required to delay travel; subjected to any condition, restriction, or requirement not imposed on other passengers; or required to provide a medical certificate if the ill passengers pose a direct threat. A direct threat is "a significant risk to the health or safety of others that cannot be eliminated by a modification

of policies, practices, or procedures, or by the provision of auxiliary aids or services." 14 C.F.R. §§ 382.3 and 382.19(c).

[25] 42 U.S.C. § 264.

[26] CDC regulations require that "the commander of an aircraft destined for a U.S. airport shall report immediately to the quarantine station at or nearest the airport at which the aircraft will arrive, the occurrence, on board, of any death or ill person among passengers or crew." 42 C.F.R. § 71.21(b). CDC regulations define "ill person" (42 C.F.R. § 71.1). 42 C.F.R. Part 70.4 requires reports of suspected cases of communicable disease on interstate flights to be made to the local public health authority with jurisdiction for the arrival airport. ICAO standards require that notification be made to air traffic control authorities. FAA and CDC have an agreement on how notifications are relayed. See *Memorandum of Agreement between the Federal Aviation Administration and the Centers for Disease Control and Prevention*, October 26, 2010.

[27] 42 C.F.R. § 71.32.

[28] According to FAA officials, any cleaning methods used to address a communicable disease threat must not negatively affect the airworthiness of the aircraft.

[29] OSHA considers occupational health and safety hazards faced by workers when prioritizing its inspections, including dangerous situations, fatalities, catastrophes, complaints, or referrals, among other criteria. This prioritization does not consider the potential for workers to spread occupational health hazards such as communicable diseases to the broader public. In the aviation system, the agency conducts new investigations based on reported safety incidents or worker allegations, according to agency officials.

[30] OSHA standards are not applicable to working conditions onboard an aircraft while it is in operation, with the exception of OSHA's standards on hazard communication, blood-borne pathogens exposure, and occupational noise exposure under a memorandum of understanding (MOU) between the agencies. An aircraft is in operation from the time it is first boarded by a crewmember, preparatory to a flight, to the time the last crewmember leaves the aircraft after completion of that flight. See *Memorandum Of Understanding Between The Federal Aviation Administration U.S. Department Of Transportation And The Occupational Safety And Health Administration U.S. Department Of Labor*, August 26, 2014.

[31] HHS has statutory responsibility for preventing the introduction, transmission, and spread of communicable diseases into the United States and between the states. 42 U.S.C. §§ 264, 265.

[32] In 2005, DHS and HHS signed an MOU outlining cooperative efforts to enhance the nation's preparedness against the introduction, transmission, and spread of quarantinable and serious communicable diseases from foreign countries into the United States and its possessions.

[33] CBP has jurisdiction over immigration and customs and—together with its DHS partner organizations—assists HHS by enforcing quarantine rules and regulations. 42 U.S.C. § 268(b); see also 42 U.S.C. § 97 (including quarantines imposed under state laws). CBP officers are trained to identify signs and symptoms of communicable disease of public health concern in travelers.

[34] According to CDC officials, implementation of such measures is extremely rare and would require cooperation with state and local public health departments.

[35] Given the spread of the Ebola epidemic, additional screening questions were also directed at travelers from Mali and Nigeria for a period of time.

[36] In general, state and local public health authorities are responsible for protecting public health within their jurisdictions, which may, at times, overlap with federal authority.

[37] During the Ebola outbreak, for example, some jurisdictions put limits on the movement of asymptomatic travelers returning from affected countries in West Africa. Likewise, monitoring ranged from in-person checkups by medical personnel in some jurisdictions to travelers from the affected countries entering data themselves through an online portal.

[38] CBP has authority under 19 U.S.C. § 1433(c) and 19 C.F.R. § 122.32 to limit the locations where aircraft entering the United States from abroad may land. CBP announced that all flights to the U.S. carrying persons who have recently traveled to, from, or through Ebola-stricken countries were to arrive at one of these five U.S. airports. 79 Fed. Reg. 63313 (Oct. 23, 2014).

[39] As of September 21, 2015, enhanced entry screening was discontinued for travelers coming to the United States from Liberia, following two incubation periods (42 days) since the last survivor tested negative for Ebola in that country. As of October 20, 2015, funneling was still in place for travelers from Guinea and Sierra Leone.

[40] For airports, we identified six high-level components through review of DOT's and HHS's *National Aviation Resource Manual for Quarantinable Diseases* and ACI's and ICAO's airport preparedness guidelines for outbreaks of communicable disease. After identifying these components, we used corroborating information about high-level components for communicable-disease preparedness that we obtained from DOT and FAA officials, a representative of CAPSCA, and some airport representatives. For airlines, we identified four components through review of IATA's emergency-response plan template for air carriers.

[41] Representatives from the remaining three airports reported that procedures for responding to communicable disease threats at their airport were contained in one document.

[42] 14 C.F.R. § 139.325. FAA provides airport operators guidance, in the form of an *Advisory Circular*, for development and implementation of an AEP. FAA AC 150/5200- 31C. The *Advisory Circular* recommends that airports structure their plans using a functional approach, which strives to avoid duplication of a planning effort for every hazard and task. Thus, it provides some guidance to airports for developing basic emergency response procedures, such as assigning responsibilities for emergency operations, which are relevant to the response to any type of emergency—including communicable disease threats.

[43] ICAO provides guidance in Annex 6 to the Chicago Convention on the type, number, location, and contents of medical supplies to be carried on aircraft, including the typical contents for a universal precaution kit—which may be used to clean up potentially infectious materials and to protect cabin crew members who are assisting potentially infectious passengers.

[44] Core capacities at airports for responding to events that may constitute a public health emergency of international concern include providing appropriate public health emergency response by establishing and maintaining a public health-emergency contingency plan. WHO, IHR (2005) – 2nd ed., Annex B.

[45] According to CDC officials, the closure of the CDC quarantine stations at Dallas/Fort Worth International and Boston Logan International airports is temporary and was a result of budget constraints.

[46] The request resulted from a series of meetings convened by DOT at the request of the aviation industry and attended by representatives from HHS, DHS, DOT, and the aviation industry to discuss standardized entry and exit screening at airports. According to DOT officials, the request did not specify which airports to extend CDC's outreach, in part because, at that time, CDC was resistant to any expansion.

[47] For the purposes of our review, we do not consider these plans to be CDRPs since they are at airports that do not currently have—or did not formerly have—a CDC quarantine station on site.

[48] CertAlert 0912. According to FAA, CertAlerts give FAA's Airports Safety and Operations Division a quick way of providing additional guidance on Airport Certification and related issues to FAA inspectors and staff.

[49] Oak Ridge Institute for Science and Education, *National Aviation Resource Manual for Quarantinable Diseases,* a report prepared for the Department of Transportation (December 2006).

[50] http://www.cdc.gov/quarantine/air/managing-sick-travelers/ebola-guidance-airlines.htm.

[51] The National Academies' Aviation Cooperative Research Program also issues guidance, such as the Transportation Research Board's *Airport Cooperative Research Program, Report 91* that recommends mitigation measures at airports and on aircraft, but is not guidance for developing a communicable disease preparedness plan.

[52] ACI and ICAO, *Airport Preparedness Guidelines for Outbreaks of Communicable Disease*, Revised (April 2009).

[53] Section F of Annex 9, subparagraph 8.16.

[54] ICAO, International Civil Aviation Organization Assembly, Res. A37-13 (November 2010).

[55] A difference filing does not necessarily signify that a member state is in noncompliance; for example, a difference filing could signify that a member state's current regulations are different in character, but achieve the same objective by other means.

[56] International Civil Aviation Organization, *State Letter EC 6/22-10/51* (June 22, 2010).

[57] In 2005, the Homeland Security Council issued the *National Strategy for Pandemic Influenza*, which identified three pillars of the National Strategy including preparedness and communication, surveillance and detection, and response and containment. In turn, the 2006 *National Strategy for Pandemic Influenza Implementation Plan* identified actions and expectations for federal agencies under each pillar to make effective international and domestic transportation decisions in order to maintain infrastructure services, mitigate adverse economic impacts, and sustain societal needs in the case of a pandemic influenza threat. The implementation plan focuses not only on transportation, but also on protecting human and animal health, law enforcement, and institutions, among other areas. Developed in response to the avian influenza threat of H5N1 that began in 2003, the strategy has not been updated to address other types of communicable diseases.

[58] In response to a requirement in the 2006 pandemic influenza implementation plan that required federal agencies to develop a strategy for border intervention that could be used during pandemics, CDC designed a strategy referred to as the Risk-Based Border Strategy (RBBS), which officials described as a flexible and scalable strategy for designing appropriate entry-screening at airports.

[59] In 2011, following the H1N1 pandemic, we found that the federal government did not activate some aspects of the pandemic influenza national strategy and implementation plan in response to H1N1 (such as critical infrastructure protection and border and trade measures) because they were not relevant given the specific characteristics of the disease outbreak. See GAO-11-632.

[60] In 2011, the White House released Presidential Policy Directive 8 (PPD-8) that aims to facilitate an integrated, all-of-nation, capabilities-based approach to preparedness. PPD-8 defined five mission areas—Prevention, Protection, Mitigation, Response, and Recovery—and directed the development of a series of policy and planning documents to enhance national preparedness. The White House, *Presidential Policy Directive 8 on National*

Preparedness (Washington, D.C.: Mar. 30, 2011). Among the planning documents, DHS has included several functional and incident-specific annexes, which describe the principles, roles and responsibilities, and coordinating structures for delivering the core capabilities to support PPD-8. The current annexes are neither targeted to the needs of the aviation sector, nor do they provide detailed information on preparing for and responding to human communicable disease incidents, specifically. For example, the Biological Incident Annex notes that specific operational guidelines, developed by respective organizations to address their unique planning considerations, will supplement this annex.

[61] A broken ticket involves a person traveling on a separate itinerary for travel between the affected country and the United States via an intermediate destination, such as from a country in Africa to a county in Europe on the way to the United States.

[62] WHO also states, in guidance to national public-health authorities in preparedness planning at designated points of entry, that individual plans need to be aligned with each other in order for tasks and actions to flow seamlessly from the national to the local level, particularly during response to public health threats at a national level. WHO, *International Health Regulations (2005): A Guide for Public Health Emergency Contingency Planning at Designated Points of Entry* (2012).

[63] China accounted for almost 1.5-million passenger arrivals in 2014.

[64] GAO-11-632.

[65] 42 C.F.R. § 71.21(b).

[66] Under FAA regulations, "No certificate holder shall require, nor may any flight crewmember perform, any duties during a critical phase of flight except those duties required for the safe operation of the aircraft." 14 C.F.R. § 121.542.

[67] 42 C.F.R. § 71.21(b). Requested information includes aircraft identification, departure airport, destination airport, estimated time of arrival, number of persons on board, number of suspected cases on board, and the nature of the public health risk, if known. HHS, Centers for Disease Control and Prevention, *For U.S. Arrivals: CDC Death and Disease Reporting Tool for Pilots* (Washington, D.C.: August 2014).

[68] CDC officials also noted that illness reporting often occurs after air travel when a passenger is diagnosed during a visit to the local health department or doctor's office. The state and local public health departments then report these cases to CDC quarantine stations.

[69] DOT officials told us that DOT's Office of Aviation Enforcement and Proceedings does not enforce any law or regulation that would protect crewmember identifying information from being accessed by other airline employees in the event of possible exposure to a communicable disease and that unless the issue affects safety, FAA regulations would not apply.

[70] 29 C.F.R. § 1910.1030(g)(2).

[71] 29 C.F.R. § 1910.1030(d)(3)(i).

[72] 29 C.F.R. § 1910.1030(d)(4).

[73] 29 C.F.R. § 1910.1030(f)(1).

[74] At least one employee of three of the four of the aviation services firms we spoke with said employers did post written notices about the Ebola outbreak in their workplace or provided copies of these notices to employees directly.

[75] Aircraft-cleaning employees with one contracted firm reported that their employer began providing better quality gloves in May 2015 after employees filed a complaint with a state occupational safety and health agency.

[76] A representative from the firm that employs the wheelchair attendants whom we spoke with said that while employees typically use anti-microbial wipes to sanitize passenger transport

equipment such as wheelchairs before they use the equipment, this step does not necessarily meet OSHA's requirements for decontamination. This representative said that airport authorities or airlines typically own passenger transport equipment, and a separate firm responsible for airport terminal cleaning is typically responsible for cleaning passenger transport equipment.

[77] None of these violations were committed by aviation services employers whose employees we spoke with. Two of the four firms with employees we spoke with have open investigations into potential violations of OSHA's blood-borne pathogens standard or analogous state standards.

End Notes for Appendix I

[1] U.S. commercial service airports accounting for 1 percent or more of total annual U.S. passenger enplanements. 49 USC 47102(10)).

[2] At one airport where the terminals are owned and operated independent of the airport authority, the airport operator suggested that we also administer the questionnaire to an operator of an international terminal, whose responses, as indicated by the airport authority, would be similar to the other international terminals.

[3] For airports, we identified six high-level components through review of DOT and HHS's *National Aviation Resource Manual for Quarantinable Diseases* and ACI and ICAO's airport preparedness guidelines for outbreaks of communicable disease. The six components are establishment of an incident command center, coordination among various stakeholders, selection and use of personal protective equipment for various stakeholders, training for various stakeholders, some protocols for responding to a threat, and protocols for decontamination. After identifying these components, we used corroborating information about high-level components to communicable preparedness collected from DOT and FAA officials, a representative of CAPSCA, and some airport representatives. For airlines, we identified four components through review of IATA's emergency-response plan template for air carriers. The four identified components are establishment of an emergency response team and designation of an emergency response center, description of the triggers that inform the level and nature of a response, activation triggers for the response team and response center, and identification of roles and responsibilities for relevant stakeholders.

[4] Airport Council International (ACI), Airlines For America (A4A), and Association of Flight Attendants (AFA).

End Notes for Appendix II

[1] The evaluations and claims of the technologies were not independently assessed by the GAO.

[2] Targeted populations are typically passengers who were recently in an area of an active outbreak.

[3] A study in the 2013 *World Health Organization (WHO) Bulletin* suggests that exit screening in regions of active outbreak is more efficient than entry screening at all possible destination airports. See Khan, K., et al, "Entry and exit screening of airline travelers during the A(H1N1) 2009 pandemic: a retrospective evaluation," *Bull World Health Organ*, vol. 90

(2013): 368-376. Our report focuses on entry screening because the United States has not carried out exit screening during disease outbreaks within the past decade. However, during the Ebola outbreak, exit screening was implemented in Ebola outbreak countries with CDC and CBP assistance.

[4] "Big Data" and data analytics can refer to analysis of large data sets—typically too large for conventional computational methods—to extract meaningful patterns and results.

[5] BioMosaic (sometimes Bio-Mosaic) entails collaboration among the CDC, several academic institutions, and data projects including BioDiaspora (now called BlueDot) and HealthMap that track disease trends. The focus on foreign-born persons is to help mitigate existing health disparities between them and U.S.-born persons. A comprehensive list of data sources is beyond the scope of this report, but includes a variety of sources including Google News and the International Air Transport Association (IATA) databases.

In: Air Travel and Communicable Diseases ISBN: 978-1-53610-188-1
Editor: Gerald Vasquez

Chapter 2

NATIONAL AVIATION RESOURCE MANUAL FOR QUARANTINABLE DISEASES*

Oak Ridge Institute for Science and Education

This document was prepared for the U.S. Department of Transportation (DOT) by the Oak Ridge Institute for Science and Education (ORIS E) through an interagency agreement with the U.S. Department of Energy (DO E). ORIS E is managed by Oak Ridge Associated Universities under DOE contract number D E-AC05-00OR22750.

THE SECRETARY OF TRANSPORTATION WASHINGTON, D.C. 20590

A MESSAGE FROM THE SECRETARY OF TRANSPORTATION

One hundred and three years ago, the Wright brothers unlocked more than the secret of flight. They unlocked the door of opportunity and growth. Since then, civil aviation has become a $900 billion industry, employing more than

* This is an edited, reformatted and augmented version of a publication prepared under contract and issued by the U.S. Department of Transportation, December 2006.

11 million people. It shrinks the world's vast distances and carries economic vitality and hope.

Unfortunately, the more than nine million flights a year that traverse our skies carry the risk of less welcome cargo: infectious diseases with the potential to disrupt our way of life and cause disastrous suffering and loss. Such quarantinable diseases include smallpox, cholera, viral hemorrhagic fevers, severe acute respiratory syndrome, and—of particular concern today—those strains **of the** influenza virus that may cause a pandemic.

In order to prevent the spread of such diseases through the airline system, we have prepared this manual. Our objective is to bolster the capabilities of airport operators, air carriers, first responders, and State and local governments, To prevent widespread transmission of quarantinable diseases, the manual provides a comprehensive guide for the organizations involved in planning for and responding to a quarantinable disease incident. We hope it will be an invaluable resource for these organizations as they develop more specific and detailed response plans to deal with emergencies.

My thanks go to Secretary of Health and Human Services Mike Leavitt and his team for working so closely with the U.S. Department of Transportation on this manual.

Mary E. Peters

THE SECRETARY OF HEALTH AND HUMAN SERVICES WASHINGTON. D.C. 20201

Our nation's ports of entry are teeming with activity. Each day, more than 5 million travelers arrive to or pass through the United States by air, sea or land. These 317 ports represent the intersection of the transportation industry. public health, and homeland security. This document is a product of collaboration among those sectors. Where our public's health is most vulnerable, such collaboration is essential.

The Department of Health and Human Services (HHS), through its Centers for Disease Control and Prevention's (CDC) Division of Global Migration and Quarantine, currently operates quarantine stations at 18 major ports of entry. Each of these 18 stations has responsibility for all other ports of entry within its assigned region of the United States. Our ports are thriving centers of commerce and trade, yet they are vulnerable to the entry of infectious disease—whether accidental or deliberate. The emergence of SARS illustrated the potential for a new disease to suddenly appear and spread, leading to widespread health, economic, and social consequences. The SARS epidemic, the outbreak of monkeypox, and the ongoing reports of avian influenza demonstrate that emerging infectious diseases are a threat to the United States.

HHS is committed to preventing the importation and spread of infectious disease in the United States. We applaud the Department of Transportation for developing this Resource Manual, which provides information of critical importance to the airport operators and local health authorities who would be called upon to respond to a traveler with a suspected infectious disease. Continued collaboration between the relevant sectors will be essential to a consistent and integrated response at our ports of entry.

Michael O. Leavitt

MANUAL OVERVIEW AND SCOPE

Introduction

The United States government has become increasingly concerned about global travel as a means for the spread of new or reemerging communicable diseases. Of particular interest is the international airline industry, which sees thousands of travelers coming into the U.S. daily through more than 130 international airports. Because of the sheer volume of travelers flowing through these airports, the potential exists for the rapid and widespread dissemination of a communicable disease within the U.S.

There are nine quarantinable diseases specified by Executive Order pursuant to the authority contained in Section 361 (b) of the Public Health Service Act. Some of these quarantinable diseases may require an immediate and large-scale response and containment strategy. For the purposes of this Manual we are focusing on the recognition and control of quarantinable diseases that require a more intensive response due to their potential for widespread impact on public health, and we have defined this recognition and control as a *quarantinable disease incident*. Most recently, concerns have been raised in this way about pandemics associated with severe acute respiratory syndrome (SARS)[†], smallpox, and avian flu, but it is reasonable to assume that responses to other quarantinable diseases would follow a similar pattern if they were deemed to present a significant public health threat.

The immediate and accurate recognition of a quarantinable disease of major public health significance is of utmost importance to the effective containment of the disease. For the most part, the recognition of the disease would be *triggered* by a combination of circumstances that would suggest that a potentially dangerous situation exists and, therefore, pertinent authorities, such as the U.S. Centers for Disease Control and Prevention (CDC), should be contacted immediately. Usually, this combination of circumstances would involve a disease alert and a travel notice along with a symptomatic traveler returning from an area for which the alert or notice had been posted. This Manual focuses on such triggered responses.

Any response and containment effort to a quarantinable disease incident will require well coordinated actions among airlines, airports, CDC, federal agencies, state and local public health departments, and first responders, all of whose efforts are essential to an efficient and effective response and containment strategy. Airlines already have their protocols and guidelines in place, as do some of the airports within the country. However, most airports do not have a manual that reviews the total effort necessary for preventing widespread transmission of quarantinable diseases throughout the U.S. This Manual provides that information. It also provides a "big picture" for those involved in both planning for and responding to a quarantinable disease incident. It does not prescribe what airport planners and responders *should do* or *have to do* at their airport. Those details are left to the individual airport planners and responders to put together based on their own logistical and jurisdictional issues.

While this Manual provides a general guide for airport quarantinable disease planning, it is important to recognize that differences in the epidemiology of quarantinable diseases require a disease-specific response. Therefore, the actions and planning recommendations outlined in this Manual may need to be updated and tailored based on novel disease characteristics or additional federal guidance as it becomes available.

[†] Note: A list of the abbreviations used within this Manual is provided in Appendix I.

Purpose

The purpose of this Manual is to be a national aviation resource outlining the response to and recovery from a quarantinable disease incident of major public health significance at a U.S. international airport. The target audience for the Manual is airlines, airports, federal response agencies and other first responders, local and state health departments, and other local and state government stakeholders that would be involved in the response to or recovery from the incident.

Scope and Assumptions

The scope and assumptions for the Manual are listed below.

1. This document is intended to provide guidance. It does not create or confer rights for or on any person, and does not operate to bind the Department of Transportation or the public. Through implementation of the National Implementation Plan for Pandemic Influenza, the U.S. Government will continue to develop guidance that might assist the aviation industry in preparedness to address communicable diseases.
2. The response activities described in this Manual would occur at international airports only when a significant public health threat exists to warrant airline and airport authorities; federal, state, and local public health agencies; and first responders to be on heightened alert and awareness for the introduction of a quarantinable disease into the U.S. on an international flight. As a result, the combination of heightened alert and awareness coupled with a potentially ill person on an international flight would trigger the high-alert response activities described in this Manual.
3. A quarantinable disease incident at a U.S. international airport had not occurred as of the writing of this Manual. Generally, CDC and other public health responders deal mostly with communicable diseases such as chickenpox, seasonal influenza, measles, and gastrointestinal illnesses. However, this does not diminish the need to plan and prepare for a quarantinable disease incident at a U.S. international airport.
4. The Pandemic and All-Hazards Preparedness Act (S. 3678, December 2006) amended the Public Health Service Act to establish the

Department of Health and Human Services (HHS) as the primary federal agency for coordinating the response to public health and medical emergencies. Therefore, under this act, the federal response to a quarantinable disease incident will likely be coordinated by the Secretary of HHS, and will be subject to the National Response Plan (NRP). Airport response plans will need to take into account the NRP structure when developing or updating their own airport response plans. The NRP structure is described in this Manual. However, it is beyond the scope of the Manual to detail exactly how individual airport response plans should incorporate the NRP structure into their own response plans. This level of detail is left to individual airport planners and responders to compile based on their own logistical and jurisdictional issues..

5. While there are nine quarantinable diseases specified by Executive Order pursuant to the authority contained in Section 361(b) of the Public Health Service Act (see Section 1 and Appendices E and F in this Manual), this Manual focuses on the recognition and control of quarantinable diseases that require a more intensive response due to their potential for widespread impact on public health (e.g., smallpox, SARS, and avian/pandemic flu). However, it is reasonable to assume that responses to other quarantinable diseases would follow a similar pattern if they were deemed to present a significant public health threat.
6. The response activities described in this Manual are for a non-bioterrorism event.
7. This Manual describes response activities at U.S. international airports.
8. The response activities described in this Manual are those that would occur at the scheduled arrival airport for an incoming international flight. In other words, the Manual does not address response activities for an airport to which the flight has been diverted. However, it should be noted that most of the response activities described in this Manual would apply at the airport to which a flight might be diverted.
9. The use of the term "airport response plan" or "airport communicable disease response plan" in this Manual refers to an airport response plan that deals with the response to a quarantinable disease at a U.S. international airport.
10. The response activities covered in this Manual apply to general aviation flights, but general aviation is not discussed in this Manual

because the response that might be associated with such flights would appear to be much smaller.

11. It is beyond the scope of this Manual to:

    a. Describe those response activities that would occur in a quarantinable disease incident in which an illness is not discovered until after the ill person has exited the airplane and been processed through the international airport.
    b. Provide specific information on local or state public health or law enforcement statutes or regulations relating to the response to or recovery from a quarantinable disease incident at a U.S. international airport. Each airport may have to address its own jurisdictional or legal issues relating to public health and law enforcement.
    c. Provide detailed information about the various types of personal protective equipment (PPE) as well as detailed instructions on its proper use. Those providing and donning surgical masks or respiratory protection should be trained in the proper types and appropriate uses of this PPE. Therefore, a certified professional should be consulted when selecting PPE and training responders on its proper use.

12. This Manual does not address:

a. Due process procedures for isolated or quarantined individuals.
b. Pre-clearance procedures in foreign countries. It addresses the response to and recovery from a quarantinable disease incident at a domestic international airport and the measures taken to prevent further dissemination of the disease. It does not address preventive measures taken at the originating foreign country or airport.
c. The importation, processing, or quarantining of animals.

13. The information contained in this Manual was current at the time of its writing.

Clarifications

For the purposes of this Manual, the terms listed below need to be clarified and understood.

Infectious and Communicable Disease

The terms *infectious disease* and *communicable disease* often are incorrectly used interchangeably. An *infectious* disease is any illness that is caused by a microorganism (e.g., virus or bacteria). A *communicable disease* is an infectious disease that is transmitted from one person to another by direct contact with an infectious individual or their discharges or by indirect means (as by a vector).

Isolation and Quarantine

Quarantine is an often misused and misunderstood term and is frequently confused with the term *isolation. Isolation* refers to the separation and restriction of movement of ill and potentially infectious persons from those who are healthy to stop the spread of disease. It is intended to stop subsequent infections by reducing exposure of well persons to a transmissible, infectious agent. *Quarantine* refers to the separation and restriction of movement of persons who, while not yet ill, have been exposed to a communicable disease and, therefore, may become infectious and transmit the disease to others.

Triggered Response and Non-Triggered Response

A *trigger* is a combination of circumstances that would suggest that a potentially dangerous situation exists and, therefore, pertinent authorities should be contacted immediately. Usually, this would involve heightened alert and awareness for a particular quarantinable disease along with a symptomatic traveler returning from an area for which a health alert had been posted. The trigger would lead to a heightened response to a potential quarantinable disease incident. This heightened response is referred to as a *triggered response*.

A *non-triggered response* could be a response to a common illness, such as gastrointestinal disorders or air sickness, and is outside the scope of this Manual. It also could be a response to a quarantinable disease incident that is not discovered until post-arrival and passenger processing. This Manual does not describe the response activities to non-triggered quarantinable disease incidents.

CDC Quarantine Stations and CDC Headquarters

CDC Quarantine Stations are within CDC's Division of Global Migration and Quarantine (DGMQ). Although they are primarily located at large international airports, they are the lead federal, public health responders or federal response coordinators at *all* seaports, airports, or land border crossings receiving international arrivals. At large domestic international airports, CDC Quarantine Station staff are the ones to whom notifications go, and they will be the ones responding to and assessing a quarantinable disease. They, in turn, may contact CDC Headquarters for notification purposes or guidance on passenger treatment, or potentially, to issue a quarantine order. Every U.S. airport falls under the jurisdiction of a CDC Quarantine Station. These are listed in Appendix A.

Manual Production

This Manual was produced with input from representatives of major airlines; international airports; airline and airport associations; federal, state, and local response agencies; state and local health departments; and other federal, state, and local public health and emergency response stakeholders. Much of the information provided in this Manual was compiled from the abovementioned entities during the commission of pandemic influenza tabletop exercises conducted for CDC at major international airports around the country. (See Appendix J for a listing of organizations that provided input and comments on this Manual.)

Contents

This Manual is divided into nine sections and has ten appendices. The first eight sections provide general concepts while the ninth section provides detailed guidance. Covered within this Manual are the following:

- The **Lead Authority**—CDC DGMQ—for the response to quarantinable disease incidents at U.S. airports.
- The role responders play in **Communicable Disease Awareness at Airports**, from disease surveillance to disease alerts.
- **Pre-Incident Preparation** to ensure an effective and efficient response to a quarantinable disease incident at an international airport.

- The **Roles and Responsibilities** of conveyance operators, airport operators, state and local governments, local healthcare facilities and support organizations, and agencies of the federal government.
- The **In-Flight Response** to a quarantinable disease incident at an international airport, including notifications, aircraft gating considerations, and responder preparations.
- The **On-Arrival Response** to a quarantinable disease incident at an international airport, including the gate response and treatment of passengers and flight crew.
- The **Post-Arrival Response** to a quarantinable disease incident at an international airport, including ill person hospitalization and isolation as well as quarantine of other passengers and flight crew.
- The **Recovery Phase** of a quarantinable disease incident at an international airport, which entails taking actions to help individuals and the community to return to normal as soon as can reasonably be done.
- **Airport Communicable Disease Response Planning** guidance for airports to use for developing their own response plans.
- **Appendices** of relevant information on:
  - CDC DGMQ Quarantine Stations,
  - CDC travel notices,
  - Personal protective equipment,
  - Legal authorities for isolation and quarantine,
  - Executive Orders on quarantinable diseases,
  - Quarantinable diseases,
  - An example of an international airport quarantine plan,
  - Incident command/unified command,
  - Abbreviations, and
  - Acknowledgments.

SECTION 1: LEAD AUTHORITY

Introduction

Title 42 United States Code Section 264 (Section 361 of the Public Health Service Act) gives the Secretary of HHS responsibility for preventing the introduction, transmission, and spread of communicable diseases from foreign countries into the United States and from one state or U.S. possession into another. This statute is implemented through regulations found at 42 CFR Parts 70 and 71. Under its delegated authority, CDC, through DGMQ, is empowered to detain, medically examine, or conditionally release persons suspected of carrying a quarantinable disease. DGMQ makes the determination as to whether an airport communicable disease incident involves a potentially quarantinable disease of public health significance.

Note: The Pandemic and All-Hazards Preparedness Act (S. 3678, December 2006) amended the Public Health Service Act to establish HHS as the primary federal agency for coordinating the response to public health and medical emergencies.

CDC Division of Global Migration and Quarantine

Under its delegated authority, DGMQ is responsible for implementing regulations necessary to prevent the introduction, transmission, or spread of communicable diseases from foreign countries into the United States. Some of the tasks undertaken to meet legal and regulatory responsibilities as they relate to the intended audiences for this Manual are to:

- Oversee the screening of arriving international travelers for symptoms of illness that could be of public health significance.
- Respond to reports of illness on board arriving aircraft.
- Provide travelers with essential health information through publications, automated fax, and the Internet.
- Collect and disseminate worldwide health data.
- Perform inspections of maritime vessels and cargos for communicable disease threats.

CDC Quarantine Stations

CDC Quarantine Stations are located at 18 ports of entry across the United States: Anchorage, Atlanta, Boston, Chicago, Detroit, El Paso (land border), Honolulu, Houston, Los Angeles, Miami, Minneapolis, New York, Newark, San Diego, San Francisco, San Juan, Seattle, and Washington. (Two new Quarantine Stations will be added in 2006 in Dallas and Philadelphia.) Each

Quarantine Station has responsibility for enforcing federal quarantine regulations at *all* ports of entry within its assigned area of jurisdiction. At ports of entry where no CDC Quarantine Station is present, the Officer in Charge and the Quarantine Medical Officer at the CDC Quarantine Station that has jurisdiction over the area will assist the state and local public health authorities and provide technical guidance and communication. (See Appendix A for a detailed listing of Quarantine Stations and their corresponding jurisdictions.)

Each Quarantine Station is staffed with an Officer in Charge, a Quarantine Medical Officer, and Quarantine Public Health Officers. The roles and responsibilities of each are as follows:

- Officer in Charge: The Officer in Charge serves as the team leader of DGMQ staff at the assigned Quarantine Station and as the recognized authority for DGMQ programs and activities at the ports of entry under his or her jurisdiction. The Officer in Charge provides guidance and direction to port partners in quarantine principles, bioterrorism preparedness, and other public health activities related to the control and prevention of communicable diseases.
- Quarantine Medical Officer: The Quarantine Medical Officer serves as a medical consultant to DGMQ staff, state and local health departments, travel industry staff, and other federal agencies directly encountering ill persons. The Quarantine Medical Officer also provides clinical, epidemiologic, and technical consultation and guidance in response to reports of illness, including threats of bioterrorism, and collaborates with local partners to apply the appropriate public health treatment.
- Quarantine Public Health Officers: Quarantine Public Health Officers conduct active and passive surveillance of travelers, flight crew, and cargo on international and domestic conveyances for indications of communicable diseases. They also direct and perform activities related to the collection, distribution, and management of medical information of immigrants, refugees, and other migrants.

Quarantinable Diseases

Under Section 361(b) of the Public Health Service Act, DGMQ has the authority to isolate and quarantine individuals or groups ill with or exposed to the following diseases (see Appendix F for more information on each disease):

1. Cholera and suspected cholera
2. Diphtheria
3. Infectious tuberculosis (TB)
4. Plague
5. Smallpox
6. Yellow fever
7. Viral hemorrhagic fevers (Lassa, Marburg, Ebola, Crimean-Congo, South American, and others not yet isolated or named).
8. Severe acute respiratory syndrome (SARS)
9. Influenza caused by novel or re-emergent influenza viruses that are causing, or have the potential to cause, a pandemic.

As noted in the Introduction, several of the diseases listed above (e.g., smallpox, SARS, and influenza with the potential to cause a pandemic) might likely result in a quarantinable disease incident. Others, such as infectious TB, would be highly unlikely to result in one.

Additionally, it is important to note that quarantine authority also resides with state and local public health officials and that some state and/or local laws may require isolation and/or quarantine for other communicable diseases (e.g., measles).

DGMQ Partnerships

DGMQ would work in collaboration with a number of federal, state, and local partners when dealing with communicable disease containment issues at an international airport.

- Federal partners include U.S. Fish and Wildlife Service (FWS), the U.S. Department of Agriculture's (USDA's) Animal and Plant Health Inspection Service (APHIS), and the following Department of Homeland Security (DHS) components: U.S. Customs and Border Protection (CBP), Immigration and Customs Enforcement (ICE), and the Transportation Security Administration (TSA) These agencies would notify DGMQ when a situation of public health interest arises. Subsequently, DGMQ staff then would assess the situation, take appropriate action, and involve CDC specialists when necessary.
- State and local partners include state and local health departments, which would be quickly notified of a quarantinable disease incident

and would be asked to provide valuable and essential assistance in the incident response.

- Airline and airport partners include international airline organizations and airport planners and responders.

HHS Partnerships

DHS is working closely with HHS. In October 2005, the two agencies signed a Memorandum of Understanding (MOU) to enhance the nation's preparedness against the introduction, transmission, and spread of quarantinable and serious communicable diseases. Specifically, this MOU addresses how travel information will be shared as well as how partners will assist with screening and handling of persons who are suspected to be ill.

SECTION 2: COMMUNICABLE DISEASE AWARENESS AT AIRPORTS

Introduction

As stated in Manual Overview and Scope, the response activities described in this Manual are those that would occur at domestic international airports only when a significant public health threat exists to warrant airline and airport authorities; federal, state, and local public health agencies; and first responders to be on heightened alert and awareness for the introduction of a quarantinable disease into the U.S. on an international air flight. This section addresses activities that would be conducted by those authorities and agencies while under that heightened alert and awareness condition.

Legal Requirement for Notification of Ill Passenger(s)

42 CFR, Section 71.21 requires that the pilot-in-command of a conveyance *immediately* report passenger illness to DGMQ. (Note: CDC's proposed rule change, "Control of Communicable Disease Proposed 42 CFR Parts 70 and 71," may alter this notification requirement.) For this purpose, an

ill passenger is defined by 42 CFR, Section 71.21 as one with either of the two conditions outlined below.

1. A temperature of 38°C (100°F) or greater, accompanied by one or more of the following: rash, jaundice, glandular swelling, or temperature persisting for two or more days.
2. Diarrhea severe enough to interfere with normal activity or work (three or more loose stools within 24 hours or a greater than normal number of loose stools).

Disease Surveillance

Surveillance means "the act of observing." It is the mechanism public health agencies use to monitor the health of their communities. In the case of disease surveillance at airports, surveillance means observing travelers for signs and symptoms of communicable diseases. There are two types of disease surveillance: passive and active.

1. Passive Surveillance: At international airports, this type of surveillance refers to information provided to CDC DGMQ without their soliciting it. An example of passive surveillance would be an airline or airport employee pointing out an ill passenger to CDC DGMQ who would then pull the passenger aside to gather more information about the passenger's physical condition and travel history. This type of surveillance would have been unsolicited by CDC DGMQ.
   It should be noted here that CBP is often the agency identifying and detaining travelers due to their passive surveillance. As outlined above, they then notify CDC DGMQ or designated local public health personnel for further medical assessment.
2. Active Surveillance: In the event of an ongoing communicable disease outbreak in a specific country or region, active surveillance measures may be implemented. The objective of this surveillance is to assess the risk that individuals arriving from affected countries or regions are carrying a potentially quarantinable illness or an illness of public health threat or significance. Examples of active surveillance would be CDC DGMQ personnel meeting arriving aircraft to visually inspect deplaning passengers for outward signs of disease or interviewing

them as they deplane to ascertain their health status and obtain their travel history.

Disease Alerts

Should one of the quarantinable diseases—or a new, unknown disease—emerge, the public health system is notified via a disease or health alert network. Throughout the world, there are several interacting disease/health alert networks. These are presented below to make airport personnel, DGMQ partners, and first responders aware of them.

- CDC's Traveler's Health: CDC's Traveler's Health program provides information on global disease outbreaks to the general public in the form of travel notices and through other information provided on their Web site. (URL: http://www.cdc.gov/travel)
- Global Outbreak and Response Network (GOARN): Administered by the World Health Organization (WHO), GOARN "is a technical collaboration of existing institutions and networks that pool human and technical resources for the rapid identification, confirmation, and response to outbreaks of international importance. The Network provides an operational framework to link this expertise and skill to keep the international community constantly alert to the threat of outbreaks and ready to respond." (URL: http://www.who.int/csr/outbreaknetwork/en/)

  GOARN is part of WHO's Communicable Disease Surveillance and Response network, which electronically updates member countries about rumored or confirmed disease outbreaks. (URL: http://www.who.int/csr/don/en)
- Global Public Health Intelligence Network (GPHIN): GPHIN is a "secure, Internet-based 'early warning' system that gathers preliminary reports of public health significance in seven languages on a real-time, 24-hour basis. This unique, multilingual system gathers and disseminates relevant information on disease outbreaks and other public health events by monitoring global media sources such as news wires and web sites. The information is filtered for relevancy by an automated process, and then is analyzed by Public Health Agency of Canada GPHIN officials. The output is categorized and made accessible to users. Notifications about public health events

that may have serious public health consequences are immediately forwarded to users." (URL: http://www.phac-aspc.gc.ca/media/nr-rp/2004/2004 gphin-rmispbk e.html)

- CDC Health Alert Notice (HAN): CDC's HAN is dedicated to strengthening the core public health infrastructure for information access, communications, and distance learning at the state and community levels. Its purpose is to "ensure that each community has rapid and timely access to emergent health information through the provision of alert notices regarding specific infectious disease threats. (URL: http://www2a.cdc.gov/han/Index.asp)

  If a HAN has been issued regarding a disease in a particular country, Quarantine Station personnel may distribute copies of the notice to each arriving traveler (or to an adult member of a family of travelers) arriving from that country. In the event of multiple flights, DGMQ may rely on its airport partners to assist in the distribution of these notices.

  (Note: HANs distributed by DGMQ to airplane passengers or flight crews differ from HANs distributed to public health professionals by CDC. The former are written in simple, easy-to-understand language and are designed for the "average" person's level of comprehension. These notices are provided in several foreign languages and contain specific information about the disease, along with a 24-hour phone number that passengers can call to receive further information.)

Travel Notices

These reports issued by CDC's Travelers' Health are based on the level of risk posed by a disease outbreak. (See Appendix B.) The four levels of travel notices are:

1. In the News: Reports sporadic cases of diseases of public health significance.
2. Outbreak Notice: Reports disease outbreaks in a limited geographic area or setting.
3. Travel Health Precaution: Reports outbreaks of greater scope that affect a larger geographic area and outline specific measures for travelers to take before, during, and after travel.

4. Travel Health Warning: Reports widespread outbreaks that have moved outside the initially affected population and may involve multiple regions or very large areas. The warning would include the precautions described above and a recommendation to reduce nonessential travel to the affected area.

Airport personnel should familiarize themselves with these travel notices to become aware of diseases in foreign countries that potentially could be brought back into the U.S.

Triggers

In terms of disease awareness at airports, a trigger is a combination of conditions that would suggest that a potentially dangerous situation exists and, therefore, pertinent authorities, such as CDC, should be contacted immediately. Usually, this combination of conditions would involve a disease alert and a travel notice along with a symptomatic traveler returning from an area for which the alert or notice had been posted. It is for this reason that airport authorities and personnel need to keep up to date on the global status of disease outbreaks.

Section 3: Pre-Incident Preparation

Introduction

There is no substitute for planning and preparation when it comes to responding to a quarantinable disease incident at an international airport. Having plans and procedures in place prior to the event will ensure an effective and efficient response to the incident, thus delaying or potentially averting the nationwide spread of a serious disease. While planning and preparing are an ongoing process, there are several tasks outlined in this section for airport quarantinable disease response planners to consider.

Authorities

It is incumbent upon all airport response personnel to know that CDC DGMQ is the lead authority (see Section 1) for the medical response to a quarantinable disease incident at an international airport, and to know how they and their organization interact with DGMQ authority. Airport response personnel should consider acquainting themselves with the Quarantine Station staff, including their roles and responsibilities, their physical location within the airport complex, and how to contact them on an "around-the-clock" basis.

Roles and Responsibilities

In addition to learning the roles and responsibilities of Quarantine Station staff, airport response personnel should know the roles and responsibilities of all entities that would respond to a quarantinable disease incident (see Section 4). Of particular note are the following pre-incident roles and responsibilities:

- Airport Operations Center, in concert with the Federal Aviation Administration (FAA), should consider having in place:
  - An airport emergency response plan that specifically addresses the response to a quarantinable disease incident.
- CDC would be expected to have in place:
  - A procedure for heightened disease monitoring at U.S. ports of entry (airports, seaports, and land border posts), working with airline and airport partners, state and local health departments, and DHS.
  - A familiarity with state and local public health authorities and emergency management agencies.
  - An active contact list with state and local public health authorities and emergency management agencies who can respond to any of the ports of entry and who can act as their designee to make medical assessments.

Worker Protection

Those involved in the response to and containment of a quarantinable disease incident potentially could be exposed to the disease in question. Therefore, these personnel need to be provided PPE appropriate for the response. PPE can include protection for eyes, face, head, and extremities. Gowns, face shields, gloves, and respirators are examples of commonly used PPE within healthcare facilities. Employees should receive training to ensure that they understand the hazards present, the necessity of the PPE, and its limitations. In addition, they should learn how to properly put on, take off, adjust, and wear PPE. Finally, employees must understand the proper care, maintenance, and disposal of PPE.

The decision about what type of PPE[‡] to use depends on the degree of communicability of the suspected illness and its route of spread. However, it is important to take appropriate precautions and don only PPE that is required for the situation. If the staff who initially board a plane for a medical assessment are "over-dressed" (e.g., wearing a biohazard suit when only a surgical mask is necessary), they could possibly frighten the passengers and flight crew and may make the initial assessment more difficult to conduct. In some situations, full PPE may be appropriate, but, in any case, it is important to explain why that level of precaution is being taken.

Pre-Incident Preparation: In-Flight Response

There are a number of tasks to consider that pertain to the in-flight response to a quarantinable disease incident (see Section 5).

- Notification Trees – Once initial notification has been made of an arriving airplane with a suspected quarantinable disease onboard, a series of other notifications begins. To ensure that proper notifications are made, airport response personnel should consider developing

[‡] Note: It is beyond the scope of this Manual to provide detailed information about the various types of PPE as well as detailed instructions on their proper use. Responding agencies already have their own PPE protocols and practices in place, and responders should adhere to what their agency prescribes. Most importantly, those providing and donning surgical masks or respiratory protection should be trained in the proper types and appropriate uses of this PPE. Therefore, a certified professional should be consulted when selecting PPE and training responders on its proper use. (For more information about PPE, please see Appendix C).

"notification trees" that show which organization(s) to contact and the methods to use (e.g., phone, radio, e-mail, etc.).

- Airplane Parking Location – After notifications have been made, it will be necessary to determine where to park the airplane. The Airport Operations Center (in coordination with FAA and CDC) should consider identifying ahead of time a location and procedure for parking an airplane during the response to a quarantinable disease incident. When considering an airplane parking location, decision makers should consider a location in which support services (e.g., fresh air, air conditioning, and electrical power) can be supplied to the airplane.
- Initial Response Team – Airport response personnel should be aware of who comprises the initial response team prior to the incident and their roles and responsibilities. They also should take into consideration "after hours" response issues, such as around-theclock notifications and delays in assembling the initial response team.
- Incident Command System – The response to a quarantinable disease incident will require the initial response team to activate and deploy its Incident Command System (ICS) (see Section 5 and Appendix H). A well planned ICS is of utmost importance to an appropriate response to a quarantinable disease incident. Therefore, responders should consider understanding the nature of ICS and Unified Command (UC) prior to an incident, and how their organization interacts within the ICS/UC structure. Additionally, they should understand the roles and responsibilities outlined in the NRP and the National Incident Management System (NIMS) (see Appendix H).
- Personal Protective Equipment – Once airport responders have been notified of the pending arrival of an airline with a suspected quarantinable disease onboard, those that will be interacting with the ill passengers will need to assemble the appropriate PPE for responding to the suspect disease. PPE should be appropriate to the situation, as determined by the responding agency's protocols. Therefore, those responders should consider having appropriate PPE accessible and have knowledge about which PPE to use for each particular disease and how to use it.

Pre-Incident Preparation: On-Arrival Response

As mentioned above, responders should know prior to the incident who the initial response team is and what PPE to use. PPE should be appropriate to the situation, as determined by the responding agency's protocols. Another task to be accomplished ahead of time is:

- Passenger Information Scripts – Passengers will look to any source for information about the unfolding events on the airplane. "Information scripts" prepared by CDC and airlines prior to an incident will help responders and the flight crew keep people accurately informed of the unfolding events on the plane.

Pre-Incident Preparation: Post-Arrival Response

Two pre-incident planning tasks that pertain to the post-arrival response to a quarantinable disease incident are:

- Identified Quarantine Facility – The airport should consider designating a "holding area" on the airport property where exposed persons can be held separately for a few hours while CDC and other public health officials evaluate a potentially quarantinable disease situation. The airport in cooperation with CDC and state and local health authorities should have identified in the airport communicable disease response plan sites for a temporary quarantine or an extended quarantine. These might be on the airport or off-airport at a site identified as part of a comprehensive community solution for dealing with possible quarantinable diseases. The Quarantine Station and the health department, with cooperation from federal and state support organizations, would be responsible for identifying the supplies and personnel needed to maintain the quarantine sites (see Section 7).
  Because state or local health authorities may issue a separate, concurrent quarantine order, these health authorities should consider having in place an identified quarantine facility and the supplies and personnel needed to manage this quarantine site.
- Pre-Designated Hospital Facilities – At some international airport cities, CDC has signed agreements with certain local hospitals–known as Memorandum of Agreement (MOA) hospitals–to manage ill

persons. An MOA hospital is a hospital that has met certain criteria and has signed a confidential agreement with CDC to manage ill travelers who are suspected of having a quarantinable disease. If there are no MOA hospitals near the airport or the pre-designated MOA hospital(s) cannot take in the ill traveler(s), responders will transfer them to another hospital designated by CDC Quarantine Station personnel or their authorized representatives in coordination with state or local emergency medical services (EMS) and public health agencies. Therefore, airport responders need to be aware that these MOA hospitals exist and that CDC will provide their names at the time of an incident. Naturally, the severity of the illness, bed availability, and security precautions for non-compliant patients need to be taken into consideration when deciding on ill traveler hospitalization.

Pre-Incident Preparation: Recovery

With regard to recovery, a pre-incident planning task is:

- Objectives of Recovery – The objectives of recovery are to assist the public, restore the environment, and restore the infrastructure. Airport responders need to have considered ahead of time the tasks required by all agencies involved in the recovery effort to accomplish these objectives.

SECTION 4: INCIDENT RESPONSE: ROLES AND RESPONSIBILITIES

Introduction

A successful response to a quarantinable disease event at an international airport will require a well-coordinated effort by conveyance operators, airport operators, state and local governments, local healthcare facilities and support organizations, and agencies of the federal government. The first step to developing and implementing an airport communicable disease response plan is to understand the roles and responsibilities of each of these authorities.

These roles and responsibilities are for ill traveler incidents during which there is suspicion that the illness may be one of the quarantinable diseases specified by Executive Order 13295 (amended) pursuant to Section 361(b) of the Public Health Service Act.

Note: The roles and responsibilities listed may not reflect those roles and responsibilities that may result from an escalating public health incident.

Conveyance Operators

Pilot-in-Command of Airplane

The roles and responsibilities of the pilot-in-command and flight crew of the airplane are to:

- Immediately report ill passenger(s) or crew members suspected of having a communicable disease to DGMQ through established protocols.[§]
- Make an initial assessment. Seek assistance from medical professionals on board the aircraft and on the ground (either airline medical staff or contract medical consultants) to make an initial assessment of the situation and communicate pertinent information to CDC personnel.
- Determine, in consultation with medical professionals, CDC, and other governmental entities, whether to proceed to the scheduled destination or divert to another airport. (Depending on the medical situation and current national security concerns, CDC, FAA, CBP, and TSA may directly influence the decision to divert.)
- Recommend what services should be staged at the airport upon arrival.
- Maintain contact with the FAA and the Airline Operations Center, which will establish and maintain contact with the CDC Quarantine Station of jurisdiction.

[§] Note: The notification procedure may be somewhat different in communicating with foreign airlines as opposed to U.S. airlines. The principal difference is that foreign airlines do not have an Airline Operations Center at a U.S. airport and, therefore, must have an airline representative meet their planes upon arrival at the domestic airport.

Airline Operations Center/Airline Representative

The roles and responsibilities of the Airline Operations Center/Airline Representative are to:

- Coordinate operations and maintain communication between the pilot-in-command of the airplane and CDC to monitor the status of an ill person.
- Provide instructions to the airplane crew, in consultation with FAA, CBP, airport operators, CDC Quarantine Station, and, if appropriate, the Federal Bureau of Investigation (FBI). (Note: Alerting the FBI is appropriate because responders cannot presume to know the nature and cause of the illness in question.)
- Coordinate with CBP and other federal partners.
- Provide assistance for an on-site crisis management team when requested to assist public health authorities. The team may include experts in communications, medical and mental health services, occupational health, environmental health, and engineer or manufacturer representatives and passenger service staff.
- Coordinate with CDC and state and local health departments on media relations.
- Help make travel arrangements and transport travelers to their final destinations when public health considerations allow.

Airport Operators

Airport Operations Center

The roles and responsibilities of the Airport Operations Center are to:

- Assist in deciding when and where the airplane should land.
- Assist with logistics.
- Provide credentials and security escorts to public health personnel and emergency responders who require access to restricted areas of the airport.
- Make appropriate notifications about the incident.
- Work with CDC and other agencies to assist in the care of passengers and flight crew if they are housed at a temporary care facility or quarantine facility at the airport.

- Coordinate with CBP and other federal partners.
- Provide transportation for passengers and flight crew to the temporary care or quarantine facility. (Proper infection control measures should be taken. See Appendix C.)
- Participate in determining a location where Incident Command (IC) or UC would operate.
- Assist with providing information to family and friends of passengers and flight crew.
- Coordinate with the FAA to provide a parking area for the aircraft.

Emergency Medical Services

The roles and responsibilities of EMS, which may require supplemental assistance from local jurisdictions, are to:

- When requested, assist public health personnel in the assessment of the ill person.
- Implement the use of infection control measures to limit transmission of communicable disease on the airplane, after landing, and during transit.
- Remove the ill person from the airplane and transport by ambulance to the designated medical facility after CBP clearance or medical parole.
- Provide first aid and other emergency medical services to ill or injured passengers or flight crew members.
- Assist the public health responders and other on-site healthcare providers, and coordinate with CDC personnel.

State and Local Governments

State and Local Health Departments

The roles and responsibilities of the state and local health departments are to:

- Perform the preliminary assessment of ill person(s) after the plane lands *if* CDC Quarantine Station staff is *not* available. (The specifics as to notification, response, assessment, and ill person disposition should be worked out between individual local and/or state health departments and the jurisdictional CDC Quarantine Station.)

- Assist in preliminary assessment of ill person(s) when CDC Quarantine Station staff is available.
- Notify state and local medical examiner or coroner if indicated.
- Coordinate, as necessary, with CDC in the issuance of quarantine and isolation orders and the management of quarantine and isolation.
- Provide staff to assist in managing a surge of ill people from the quarantine site arriving at a hospital (or hospitals).
- Assist, as needed, federal public health agencies with setting up a medical clinic at the quarantine site.
- Provide guidance to designated hospitals and/or the quarantine site medical clinic on the clinical and diagnostic management of ill people, including assisting with arrangements for laboratory testing at local or state public health laboratories or at CDC.
- Prepare strategies for mental health interventions for ill persons and persons who have been exposed and are under quarantine, their families, and service providers.
- Assist emergency management agencies, if needed, in planning for and activating a temporary care facility and quarantine facility.
- Provide clinical and public health information to local healthcare providers and the public.
- Provide information and recommendations to local and state authorities.
- Coordinate with the IC/UC on media relations.
- Coordinate with CDC Quarantine Station on recommendations and guidance as needed.

State and Local Emergency Management Authorities

The roles and responsibilities of the state and local emergency management authorities are to:

- Assist and support state and local public health authorities with financial and other measures if temporary care and quarantine facilities are activated.
- Work with state and local health departments to support the planning and preparation activities to operate temporary care and quarantine

facilities at each international and domestic airport, seaport, and land border crossing.
- Seek assistance from the Federal Emergency Management Agency (FEMA) when appropriate.

Law Enforcement Agencies

The roles and responsibilities of law enforcement agencies are to:

- Provide security for the response staging area and control access to and from the airplane and the airport.
- Escort agency representatives into and out of IC and the airport as needed.
- Provide representatives to IC.
- Maintain order.
- Assist in and expedite the transfer of ill persons and clinical materials for evaluation and treatment.
- Enforce required actions (e.g., transportation) for ill persons or persons who have been exposed to an illness if any such persons are uncooperative. (Proper infection control measures should be taken. See Appendix C.)

Local Healthcare Facilities and Support Organizations

Healthcare Facilities

The roles and responsibilities of healthcare facilities are to:

- Isolate ill persons when medically indicated.
- Institute infection control measures to limit the spread of quarantinable diseases. This may include isolation of ill persons and use of PPE by staff and visitors when medically indicated.
- Evaluate and treat referred ill persons. This includes obtaining specified diagnostic specimens and assuring the specimens are promptly and safely transported to designated laboratories. It also includes assessing the need for and providing prescription medications for the ill persons.
- Evaluate exposed people if they develop illness signs or symptoms while in quarantine.

- Provide clinical and laboratory information to federal, state, and local public health authorities.
- Work with public health authorities on media relations.

Support Organizations

A number of different support organizations, including non-government organizations, would be brought in to provide support services to people exposed to the illness (quarantined individuals), as well as to service providers. Such support services may be modified depending on the nature of the quarantine to protect volunteers. Support services include, but are not limited to:

- Meals (including special meals for those under dietary restrictions)
- Beverages (including sterile water and formula for infants)
- Eating utensils, plates and napkins
- Tables and chairs
- Cots and bedding
- Space heaters and fans
- Portable toilet facilities and toiletries
- Hand-washing facilities
- Portable showering facilities
- Parent-child needs (e.g., diapers)
- Telephones
- Means of communicating with family
- Television, movies, and radio
- Internet access and email
- Reading materials and games
- Public address system
- Interpreter services
- Spiritual support
- Mental health support

Federal Government

Centers for Disease Control and Prevention (CDC)

The roles and responsibilities of CDC are to:

- Authorize the temporary detention, through federal order as necessary, of passengers and flight crew for appropriate evaluation and response to reports of illness.
- Issue federal quarantine orders if warranted.
- Notify and collaborate with other federal, state, and local agencies when ill travelers have been detained or paroled into the United States for evaluation or treatment for communicable diseases.
- Arrange or assist in the medical evaluations of ill travelers and determine the need for public health interventions.
- Provide advice and guidance to the public health responders, including state and local public health authorities, in implementing quarantine measures and caring for ill persons and persons who have been exposed to the illness.
- Obtain information on ill and exposed travelers (e.g., demographics, contact information, travel itinerary, illness history, and medical status) and the conveyance (number of passengers, manifest availability).
- Communicate with other federal, state, and local response and public health partners regarding the ill person's medical treatment.
- Participate in the management of media relations, in collaboration with state and local health departments and information officers from other response partners.
- Work with the Department of State and WHO to provide information about ill international travelers to ministries of health at their place of origin and at intermediate destinations.
- Work with the Department of State, as necessary, to notify applicable foreign consulates or embassies that their foreign nationals have been detained for evaluation or treatment of a quarantinable disease.
- Assist in the development of occupational health and infection control guidelines for the Federal Inspection Site (FIS) at ports of entry.
- Rescind federal quarantine orders when the public health situation allows.

Department of Homeland Security

DHS leverages resources within federal, state, and local governments, coordinating the transition of multiple agencies and programs into a single, integrated agency focused on protecting the American people and their homeland. At international airports, the following DHS components play a role in the response to a quarantinable disease incident.

Customs and Border Protection

The roles and responsibilities of CBP are to:

- Support initial entry screening of international travelers (using up-to-date information provided by CDC) for the purposes of identifying potentially infected travelers.
- Provide enforcement resources during a medical response until the appropriate enforcement agency arrives at the plane.
- For international flights, meet the conveyance and prevent disembarkation until CDC or their designated alternate arrives. (TSA has concurrent authority.)
- Escort medical personnel and other emergency responders on to the aircraft.
- Notify the appropriate CDC Quarantine Station to initiate their medical assessment before releasing detained passengers.
- Assist CDC in identifying travelers at risk and those suspected of having been in contact with an ill person by providing passenger customs declarations, Advance Passenger Information System (APIS) data, and other sources of traveler information in response to a specific request by CDC.
- Assist CDC by providing information for use in locating people suspected of having contact with an ill person.
- Parole, if necessary, ill non-U.S. citizens and non-permanent residents (e.g. nonimmigrant students, workers, etc.) into the United States if public health interventions are indicated.
- Assist CDC, as necessary and as resources permit, in distributing health information at ports of entry.
- Assist in the development of occupational health and infection control guidelines for the federal inspection site at ports of entry.

Immigration and Customs Enforcement

ICE is an investigative agency of DHS. Specific ICE officers are authorized under the Public Health Service Act to:

- Assist CDC in the enforcement of quarantine and isolation.

Transportation Security Administration

If the Secretary of DHS determines that a situation involving a communicable disease presents a security threat, TSA may, under various authorities within the Aviation Transportation Security Act and the Homeland Security Act, request that FAA either:

- Direct a flight destined for the U.S. from landing in the U.S. or direct the flight to land at a specified airport in the U.S. that is equipped to examine and handle a suspected infectious person on the aircraft until CDC or their designated alternate arrives.

Federal Aviation Administration (FAA)

The roles and responsibilities of FAA are to:

- Provide air traffic control services and handling priority as required to permit safe and expeditious arrival and landing at the destination airport.
- Provide taxi instructions to a parking location designated by competent authority to effectively implement public health intervention in response to illnesses on board.
- Establish and assist with enforcement of temporary flight restrictions where requested by competent authority in the interest of public health and safety.
- At the request of TSA, direct a flight destined for the U.S. from landing in the U.S. or direct the flight to land at a specified airport in the U.S. that is equipped to examine and handle a suspected infectious person on the aircraft.

SECTION 5: INCIDENT RESPONSE: IN-FLIGHT

Introduction

Federal law requires the pilot-in-command to *immediately* contact the appropriate CDC Quarantine Station about an illness or death on an aircraft (see Section 2). The pilot can do this through either the FAA or the airline's dispatch center, which would then notify the jurisdictional CDC Quarantine Station. This notification would then trigger other notifications and preparations prior to the arrival of the aircraft. Notifications among responding agencies to a quarantinable disease incident on an international aircraft should be timely and redundant. This section describes the notifications, preparations, and responsibilities of all involved entities.

Notifications: Airports with an on-Site CDC Quarantine Station

The notification process for international airports with an on-site CDC Quarantine Station differs slightly from those airports that do not have a Quarantine Station. The difference is mainly in the delegation of authority to other on-site responders at non-CDC Quarantine Station airports. Listed below are the notifications for the in-flight response to a quarantinable disease incident on an international flight at airports with an on-site CDC Quarantine Station. Please note that, in this list, there are built in redundancies to ensure proper notification of all responding entities. Airport communicable disease response planners may wish to reduce or eliminate these redundancies as they see fit for their particular airport operation.

- Pilot-In-Command notifies:
  - Airline dispatch center
  - FAA
  - CDC Quarantine Station
- CDC Quarantine Station notifies:
  - CBP
  - Airport police/Fire Department/EMS Dispatch Center
  - State and local public health departments
  - Healthcare facility (depending on the nature of the event)
  - CDC headquarters (depending on the nature of the event)
  - FBI
- FAA notifies:
  - CDC Quarantine Station
  - Airport Operations
  - CBP
  - TSA
- Airport Police/Fire Department/EMS Dispatch Center notifies:
  - Airport operations center
  - CDC Quarantine Station

    - CBP
    - TSA
- Airport Police/Fire Department/EMS notifies:
    - CDC Quarantine Station
    - Airport operations center
- Airline Operations Center/Airline Representative notifies:
    - CDC Quarantine Station
    - Airport police/fire department/EMS
    - CBP
    - TSA
- CBP notifies:
    - CDC Quarantine Station
- TSA notifies:
    - CBP

Notifications: Airports without an On-Site CDC Quarantine Station

At international airports without an on-site CDC Quarantine Station, the response to a quarantinable disease incident on an international flight relies on on-site responders who have been delegated authority by the jurisdictional Quarantine Station to act on its behalf. Airports without a Quarantine Station should notify the jurisdictional Quarantine Station and the local health department for both domestic and international flights. Listed below are the notifications for the in-flight response at airports without an on-site CDC Quarantine Station. Please note that, in this list, there are built in redundancies to ensure proper notification of all responding entities. Airport communicable disease response planners may wish to reduce or eliminate these redundancies as they see fit for their particular airport operation.

- Pilot-In-Command notifies:
    - Airline dispatch center
    - FAA
    - Jurisdictional CDC Quarantine Station
- Jurisdictional CDC Quarantine Station notifies:
    - CBP
    - Airport police/Fire department/EMS Dispatch Center

- State/local health department
- Healthcare facility
- CDC Headquarters
- FBI
- FAA notifies:
    - Jurisdictional CDC Quarantine Station
    - CBP
    - Airport police/fire department/EMS dispatch center
    - TSA
- Airport Police/Fire Department/EMS Dispatch Center notifies:
    - Airport police/fire department/EMS
    - Airport operations center
    - Jurisdictional CDC Quarantine Station
    - CBP
    - TSA
- Airport Operations Center/Airline Representative notifies:
    - Jurisdictional CDC Quarantine Station
    - Airport police/fire department/EMS
    - CBP
    - TSA
- CBP notifies:
    - Jurisdictional CDC Quarantine Station
- TSA notifies:
    - CBP

Other Notification Considerations

In addition to the responders listed in the notifications above, the entities listed below may be considered in notification lists for airport response planning:

- City/County Responders
    - Emergency Management Agency
    - EMS
    - Law enforcement
    - Communicable disease specialist/controller

  - Medical laboratory
  - Public information officers
  - Non-governmental agencies
- State Responders
  - Emergency Management Agency
  - Health department
  - Law enforcement
  - Communicable disease specialist/controller
  - Medical laboratory
  - Public information officers

Preparation for the Arrival of the Aircraft

Preparing for the arrival on an international flight with a quarantinable disease incident on board involves three activities: deciding where to park the aircraft, assembling the initial response team, and preparing for the arrival of the ill person(s).

Parking the Aircraft

The nature of the event and the scope of the anticipated response will dictate where to park the aircraft. Three options for parking the aircraft are:

- Park the aircraft at its assigned gate. Airport operator in coordination with the FAA, CBP and CDC will decide where the aircraft will be parked. The advantages of parking the aircraft at its assigned gate are that responders will have easy access to the ill person(s) and that, should the incident be a minor one, travelers will be able to disembark quickly. The disadvantage is that the infected person(s) may have the potential to contaminate the passenger boarding bridge and gate area. Additionally, if the incident turns out to be a major event, it will tie up the gate for hours, and may be more difficult to manage.
- Park the aircraft at a secure, remote gate. The advantage of parking the aircraft at a secure, remote gate is that responders will have unconstrained access to the ill person(s). The disadvantages are that the remoteness of the gate could prevent the responders from getting to it and exiting it quickly and that, should the incident be a minor

one, the plane may have to be moved to its original gate or an alternate gate at the airport.

- Isolate the aircraft on the airport ramp. One advantage of isolating the aircraft on the airport ramp is it helps prevent the spread of a possible quarantinable disease. Another advantage is that responders will have access to passengers and flight crew. The disadvantages are that special equipment may be needed for responders to board the plane and that the remoteness of the area could prevent the responders from getting to it and exiting it quickly. Another disadvantage is that, should the incident be a minor one, the plane may have to be moved to its original gate or an alternate gate at the airport.

When considering an airplane parking location, decision makers should consider a location in which support services (e.g., fresh air, air conditioning, and electrical power) can be supplied to the airplane.

Passenger Considerations

Holding people on an airplane or on airport grounds presents some sensitive issues to consider:

- Maintaining the health of the "well" passengers and flight crew – Inadequate ventilation, insufficient bathroom facilities, and the potential for deep vein thrombosis from sitting for long periods of time pose health risks for "well" passengers and flight crew. It is important that the Quarantine Station or public health personnel evaluate the ill person(s) in an expeditious manner and remove them promptly if warranted.
- Keeping the passengers informed – Passengers will look to any source for information about the unfolding events on the airplane. Responding agencies need to assist and encourage the flight crew to keep passengers informed and calm.
- Keeping the situation under control – The public health officer who enters the plane should ask the flight attendants to keep everyone seated until the medical evaluation is made. Should "well" passengers become unruly, the public health officer should request assistance from the jurisdictional law enforcement agency.
- Informing family members and those waiting for the airplane – Airlines need to keep those waiting for the airplane informed about

what is occurring on the airplane. Some airports/airlines have waiting areas for the families and friends awaiting passengers and flight crew.

Assembling the Initial Response Team

The initial response team for a quarantinable disease incident at an international airport should be assembled and waiting for the aircraft.* This team should have gathered as much information from the airline ahead of time as possible in order to make an informed judgment as to the type of disease(s) they may encounter and to have the necessary PPE on hand to make an initial screening and diagnosis.

At international airports with an on-site CDC Quarantine Station, the initial response team would comprise:

- CDC Quarantine Station personnel
- CBP
- Airport police/fire department/EMS
- Local public health department

At international airports without an on-site CDC Quarantine Station, the initial response team would comprise:

- CBP (Acting Lead in consultation with CDC Quarantine Station)
- Local public health department
- Airport police/fire department/EMS

As noted in Section 3, Pre-Incident Preparation, all airport response personnel should be aware of the make-up and roles and responsibilities of the initial response team prior to the incident. They also should take into consideration "after hours" response issues, such as around-theclock notifications, and delays in assembling the initial response team.

*Note: In the "best case" scenario, notifications would be made in a timely manner to all of the appropriate authorities. However, there are instances when notifications are late, thereby delaying the assemblage of the initial response team. Responders need to keep in mind the health and safety of both the ill person(s) and the well passengers and flight crew. The response to the quarantinable disease incident needs to be swift and effective. Ill person disposition should not be delayed while waiting for the entire response team to assemble.

Incident Command System

If a quarantinable disease is suspected, the initial response team would activate and deploy their ICS. The ICS is a standardized on-scene incident management concept designed specifically to allow responders to adopt an integrated organizational structure equal to the complexity and demands of any single incident or multiple incidents without being hindered by jurisdictional boundaries. (See Appendix H for more detailed information on IC or UC.)

Preparing for the Arrival of Ill Passenger(s)

In addition to the initial response team, other entities may need to prepare for the arrival of not only an ill person or persons, but also the treatment of exposed people (i.e., quarantine). Those entities and their corresponding roles and responsibilities are:

- Local Healthcare Facilities
    - Prepare for the arrival of ill people who may need medical care under isolation; and
    - Develop strategies with the state and local health departments to deliver care to people under quarantine who need medical services.
- State and Local Governments
    - Prepare for on-site or remote consultation to determine medical and public health treatment of the ill person(s) and possible quarantine of people who may have been exposed to the illness;
    - Inform local agency partners and prepare for the enforcement of quarantine in a temporary-care facility for people who were exposed to the ill person; and
    - Develop strategies with the local healthcare facility to deliver care to people under quarantine who need medical services.
- Federal Government
    - Develop strategies to isolate the ill person(s) and to quarantine people exposed to the ill person;
    - Prepare for the enforcement of isolation and quarantine measures for the arriving travelers and conveyance at the port of entry; and
    - Prepare to request and collect passenger locating information.

SECTION 6: INCIDENT RESPONSE: ON ARRIVAL

Introduction

The on-arrival response to a quarantinable disease incident at an international airport poses a "balancing act" for the initial response team and the airline. While responders want to take as much time as necessary to interview the ill travelers on board the aircraft and make an informed diagnosis, they also must take into consideration the hundreds of other passengers and flight crew who may or may not have been exposed to a potentially dangerous disease and who want to disembark as soon as possible to return to their homes or continue their travels, and the airline that needs to put the aircraft back in service.

Planeside Response

Once the plane has been parked, two activities will occur:

- CDC Quarantine Station personnel or their designated alternate (e.g., local health department) will board the plane and be directed to the ill person(s). Before reaching the ill person(s), they may don PPE appropriate for the anticipated illness. Once they reach the ill persons, they will assess the symptoms, take a travel history, and make an initial determination and treatment. (See "Treatment of Ill People" below.)
- The remaining people should have been notified prior to the plane being parked that there is an ill person on board requiring medical evaluation before anyone else can be cleared for deplaning. This announcement should be made again as the medical responders are boarding the plane, and it should be made periodically during the assessment. However, note that, the longer the assessment takes, the more anxious the remaining people will become. Therefore, the appropriate law enforcement authority may be asked to board the plane to maintain order. (See "Treatment of Exposed People" below.)

Treatment of Ill People

The response to ill or exposed passengers and flight crew on the aircraft depends on the initial determinations and diagnosis of those assessing the ill person(s). The following "if-then" conditional statements outline how the passengers and flight crew will be managed:

1. If the ill person is assessed and determined to have an illness that is not of public health significance (e.g., diabetes), then:

- The ill person, upon receiving a planeside medical clearance by CDC or their designated alternate, will be transported to a healthcare facility, if necessary.
- The other passengers and flight crew will be released to continue regular federal clearing processing.

2. If the ill person is assessed and is suspected of having an illness of public health significance but not one that would pose a threat to other people on the aircraft or in the community (e.g., malaria), then:

- The ill person, upon receiving a planeside medical clearance by CDC or their designated alternate, will be transported to a healthcare facility for further evaluation or treatment.
- The other passengers and flight crew will be released to continue CBP processing.

3. If the ill person is assessed and is suspected of having a *non-quarantinable illness* (e.g., measles) that could pose a threat to other people on the aircraft or in the community then:

- The ill person will be isolated and provided a surgical mask, if the person can tolerate wearing one. If they cannot wear a surgical mask they will be instructed to practice respiratory/cough etiquette (see the following CDC web site at: www.cdc.gov/flu/professionals/infectioncontrol/resphygiene.htm) and to use good hand hygiene.
- Other responders and the designated healthcare facility (local hospital) will be alerted to apply appropriate precautions (e.g., PPE).
- The ill person may be transported under appropriate isolation measures to a local hospital.
- Notifications will be made to CDC Headquarters, healthcare facilities, and state and local health departments.

- Health alert notices about the disease may be distributed to the passengers and flight crew.
- Locator information may be collected from some or all of the remaining "well" passengers and flight crew before releasing them. CDC will request this passenger information from CBP, if needed.

4. If an ill person is assessed and suspected of having a *quarantinable illness* (e.g., pandemic influenza), then:

- The ill person will be isolated from others and provided a mask if available, or tissues, if this has not been done already and if the person does not have breathing difficulties.
- Other responders and designated healthcare facilities will be alerted to apply appropriate precautions, including PPE.
- The ill person will be transported under appropriate isolation measures to a designated healthcare facility after clearing CBP processing and/or temporary parole.
- Notifications will be made to CDC Headquarters, healthcare facilities, and state and local health departments.
- All people who may have been exposed to the ill person will be identified, and contact information for each will be collected.
- An order for quarantine will be issued by CDC.
- Quarantine plans for the exposed passengers and flight crew will be implemented (see Section 7).
- State and local support organizations will be alerted.
- Appropriate agencies will coordinate IC/UC, ensuring consistency and accuracy.

Treatment of Exposed People

As seen above, when an ill person is assessed and suspected of having an illness that could pose a threat to other people on the airplane or in the community, those remaining will be asked to provide contact information before being released or they will be quarantined. In the case of quarantine, the information will be collected at the quarantine site. Quarantine is covered in Section 7.

Information Given to Exposed People

If the exposed people are going to be allowed to deplane and not be quarantined, they will be provided with health information instructing them about the signs and symptoms of the disease and what to do if they observe any of these signs and symptoms in themselves.

Information Collected from Exposed People

Both the airlines and CDC learned from the SARS experience that tracing exposed passengers and flight crew is a very difficult task. Fortunately, they have worked together to improve the methods for collecting information from exposed passengers and flight crew. Several methods of collecting passenger and flight crew information are described below.

- Passenger Locator Cards: The passenger locator card was developed by CDC with input from the airlines to collect contact information from passengers in a machine-readable format. Using a targeted approach, CDC will identify countries where exposure to quarantinable disease is most likely and then stock the Passenger Locator Cards, as well as Health Alert Notices, on flights arriving from these countries. Using this approach, passenger information can be collected before deplaning.
- Immigration Forms: Non-U.S. citizens and non-permanent residents with certain exceptions (e.g. Canadian citizens) must fill out CBP Form I-94 or I-94W, Arrival/Departure Record. A crewmember must complete CBP Form I-95, Crewman Landing Permit. These forms provide information about the passengers' or crewmembers' nationalities and their travel itineraries within the U.S.
- eAPIS: CBP's Electronic Advance Passenger Information System (eAPIS) online transmission system collects passenger information for arriving and departing flights. For international flights arriving in the U.S., passenger information needs to be submitted in advance of an aircraft's arrival.

Because most international flights carry hundreds of people, CDC may call on the airline or CBP to assist them in obtaining the abovementioned information.

SECTION 7: INCIDENT RESPONSE: POST-ARRIVAL

Introduction

The post-arrival response to a quarantinable disease incident at an international airport is multi- faceted and depends on the nature of the incident and the scope of the response. As seen in the previous section, in an event of low public health significance, the ill person is assessed and, if necessary, hospitalized, and the remaining passengers and flight crew are released. In an event of high public health significance, the ill person is assessed and hospitalized, and the remaining passengers and flight crew either are released after providing contact information or are quarantined. Contact information was discussed in the previous section. This section covers hospitalization of ill persons and quarantine of exposed passengers and flight crew.

Hospitalization of the Ill Persons

Once the initial response team has decided to hospitalize the ill person(s), there are three considerations that need to be addressed:

1. To which hospital do the ill persons go?
2. Under whose charge are they going?
3. What happens if they don't want to go?

Memoranda of Agreement Hospitals

The answer to the first question is that EMS would take ill people to one of CDC's pre-designated MOA hospitals for that particular airport. An MOA hospital is a hospital that has met certain criteria and has signed a confidential agreement with CDC to manage ill travelers who are suspected of having a quarantinable disease. If there are no MOA hospitals near the airport or the pre-designated MOA hospital(s) cannot take in ill travelers, responders will transfer them to another hospital designated by CDC Quarantine Station personnel or their authorized representative(s) in coordination with state or local EMS and public health agencies.

Naturally, the severity of the illness, bed availability, and security precautions for noncompliant patients need to be taken into consideration when deciding on hospitalization of ill persons. In a life-threatening situation, responders will take ill travelers to the closest hospital that can treat them.

CBP

All travelers on international flights must go through the federal clearance process before entering the U.S. Therefore, they are under federal authority and control until they have been released into the country. If necessary, CBP may provide planeside clearances, if admissible, or temporary parole of ill people to allow for disembarkation from the passenger boarding bridge directly to an awaiting ambulance on the tarmac. The advantage of this protocol is that it would lessen the potential of exposure to other people within the federal inspection area and the airport terminal.

Recalcitrant Travelers

Ill travelers may insist that they are not ill enough to require hospitalization. Should this case arise, CDC Quarantine Station personnel or their authorized representative(s) will:

- Consult with state and local health authorities and issue a federal isolation order.
- Call on local, state, or federal law enforcement to enforce the federal order.

Should an ill traveler resist an isolation order or attempt to flee, CDC Quarantine Station personnel may, pursuant to authorities contained in the Public Health Service Act, request that state and local authorities or federal law enforcement detain the individual and provide security during medical evaluation and treatment.

Quarantine

Quarantine and isolation represent two ways of trying to contain a quarantinable disease within a community. Historically, both methods have been used, most recently during the 2003 SARS epidemics in which China, Hong Kong, Singapore, and Canada issued quarantine orders. There has not been any large-scale quarantine incident in the United States in recent history. Regardless of whether quarantine or isolation is used, the governing authority over the quarantine or isolation, whether it be local, state, or federal, has an obligation to provide adequate healthcare, food and water, and a means of communication with family and friends.

The terms *isolation* and *quarantine* often are used interchangeably, but they have very different meanings and serve different purposes. CDC's "Fact Sheet: Isolation and Quarantine" (URL: http://www.cdc.gov/ncidod/dq/sars facts/isolationquarantine.pdf and Appendix D) explains the two terms in the following way:

- *Isolation* refers to the separation of people who have a specific infectious illness from those who are healthy and to the restriction of their movement to stop the spread of that illness. Isolation allows for the focused delivery of specialized health care to people who are ill, and it protects healthy people from getting sick. People in isolation may be cared for in their homes, hospitals, or designated healthcare facilities. Isolation is a standard procedure used in hospitals today for patients with TB and certain other infectious diseases. In most cases, isolation is voluntary; however, many levels of government (federal, state, and local) have basic authority to compel isolation of sick people to protect the public.
- *Quarantine* refers to the separation and restriction of movement of people who, while not yet ill, have been exposed to an infectious agent and therefore may become infectious. Quarantine of exposed people is a public health strategy, like isolation, that is intended to stop the spread of infectious disease. Quarantine is medically very effective in protecting the public from disease.

Authority to Quarantine

Section 1 explained that CDC DGMQ is the lead authority for the response to a quarantinable disease incident at an international airport. Under this authority, DGMQ is empowered to detain, medically examine, or conditionally release people suspected of carrying a quarantinable disease. Therefore, in an incident where a traveler on an international flight is suspected of being ill with a quarantinable disease and quarantine of the remaining passengers and flight crew is indicated, *CDC will issue the initial order to quarantine the exposed passengers and flight crew*. However, because state and local health authorities may have concurrent legal power to order quarantine, secondary orders to quarantine may come from these entities. (See "Fact Sheet: Legal Authorities for Isolation and Quarantine" in Appendix D.)

Change in Quarantine Authority

Depending on the scope of the incident and the nature of the disease, quarantine may last from a few days to a few weeks. In short-term quarantines, federal authorities will maintain their authority. However, in long-term quarantine situations, they may transition the authority to state and local governments.

Quarantine Planning

As noted above, CDC will be the lead authority for quarantining exposed passengers and flight crew. However, because the quarantine may take place on airport grounds or within the local community, CDC may consult with airport, state, and local organizations to select and prepare the quarantine site and manage the overall quarantine. Therefore, these organizations need to understand state and local quarantine laws, prescribed responsibilities, and requisite documentation. They also need to be prepared in advance for a quarantine incident within their jurisdictional boundaries. This planning and preparation includes:

1. Identifying a secure location and requisite lodging for quarantine.
2. Identifying the staff needed to sustain, enforce, and provide services to quarantined individuals and from where this staff will come.
3. Identifying the supplies needed to sustain quarantine and from where these supplies will come.
4. Identifying the medical and mental health needs of the quarantined population and how these needs will be met.
5. Identifying the special needs (e.g., children, pregnant women, people with disabilities, and differing cultures and religions.) of the quarantined population and how these needs will be met.
6. Identifying the support organizations available to assist in managing quarantine.
7. Identifying the financial needs for managing quarantine.
8. Addressing the legal needs for managing quarantine (e.g., due process protections for quarantined passengers and flight crew).
9. Addressing media and public information issues [e.g., setting up a Joint Information Center (JIC)].

Quarantine Planning Considerations

The preceding paragraph lists nine steps to planning for quarantine (i.e., developing a quarantine plan). Outlined below are considerations when developing this plan. (See Appendix G for an example of an international airport quarantine plan.)

- Site/Location: There are several considerations for selecting a quarantine site:
    - Security: The site needs to have containment boundaries (e.g., fences or walls) to keep people in and keep people out.
    - Size: The site needs to be large enough to accommodate at a minimum the number of passengers, flight crew, and staff that would be on the largest capacity airplane that might visit the airport. When considering how many people would be quarantined, take into account the largest (in terms of passenger and flight crew capacity) international flight arriving at the airport.
    - Accessibility: The site needs to be readily accessible to security forces, medical personnel, and suppliers.
    - Comfort: Because quarantine may be a long-term situation, the comfort—both physical and mental—of the quarantined passengers and flight crew as well as staff needs to be taken into consideration.
- Staff: Quarantine staff need to perform a variety of medical, mental health, occupational, and spiritual functions. Also, quarantine is an around-the-clock activity, so different shifts of staff need to be taken into consideration.
- Supplies: When considering supply needs, take into account that quarantine may extend over a week, or longer depending on the incubation period. Types of supplies range from medical to food to occupational needs for passengers who want to work during quarantine.
- Medical Needs: Quarantined people may have medical needs unrelated to the disease for which they have been quarantined.
- Special Needs: The quarantine population will be a diverse group of people with varying religious and cultural needs. Things to take into consideration are communication issues, religious issues, and dietary

needs. Have foreign-language interpreters on call to deal with non-English speaking passengers.

- Support Organizations: There are non-governmental organizations available to provide services in coordination with the local emergency management agency. These support services may be modified, depending on the nature of the quarantine.
- Financial Needs: One of the big questions about quarantine is who is going to pay for it. While the answer sometimes lies in a "gray zone," planners can help determine payment obligations by tracking all expenditures and costs before, during and after quarantine.
- Public Information Issues: The media will be ever present to keep a spotlight on quarantine.

Ending Quarantine

Quarantine is *usually* ended when two disease incubation periods have passed with no signs or symptoms of the quarantinable disease in the quarantined community. The incubation period includes the period between a person having acquired the infectious agent, becoming infected, and becoming symptomatic. This process varies for different diseases. The order to end quarantine will come from the respective entity or entities exercising jurisdiction over the quarantine.

Just as there are things to consider when instituting quarantine, there are several considerations to take into account when ending quarantine:

- Rebooking Flights: Some quarantined people had planned further travels before they were quarantined. Their continuing travel needs to be considered.
- Traveler Briefing: The quarantined passengers and flight crew have just gone through a long ordeal. They may be hounded by the media for details or questioned by friends and families about it. CDC, public information officers, and public health officers should brief them ahead of time to help them cope with these inquiries.

Some of the end-of-quarantine activities involve the recovery phase of quarantine. These activities will be discussed in the next section.

SECTION 8: INCIDENT RESPONSE: RECOVERY

Introduction

The information provided in this section is taken from the NRP and the DHS Office of State and Local Government Coordination and Preparedness, Universal Task List (UTL): Version 2.1 (URL: http://www.ojp.usdoj.gov/odp/docs/UTL2 1.pdf).

What Is Recovery?

Recovery entails taking actions to help individuals and the community to return to normal as soon as can reasonably be done. The NRP defines recovery as "the development, coordination, and execution of service- and site-restoration plans and the reconstitution of government operations and services through individual, private-sector, nongovernmental, and public assistance programs."

With regard to a quarantinable disease incident at an international airport, recovery may entail only cleaning an aircraft and rebooking travelers. Or, in a major public health incident, it may entail a large-scale effort, such as decontaminating a quarantine site, re-stocking medical and social supplies, providing mental health services, and rebooking passenger flights, among other things.

Objectives of Recovery

As discussed in the UTL, there are three objectives for the recovery mission:

- **Assist the public** – Help individuals directly impacted by an incident to return to pre-incident levels, where feasible. Sub-objectives of this objective are to:

    1. Provide long-term healthcare.
    2. Educate the public.
    3. Provide social services.

- **Restore the environment** – Reestablish or bring back to a state of environmental or ecological health the water, air, and land, and the interrelationship that exists among and between water, air, and land and all living things. Sub-objectives are to:
    1. Conduct site cleanup.
    2. Dispose of materials.
    3. Conduct site remediation.
    4. Restore natural resources.
- **Restore the infrastructure** – Restore the infrastructure in the affected communities in order to return to pre-incident levels, where feasible. Sub-objectives are to:
    1. Reconstitute government services.
    2. Rebuild property.

With regard to applicability to a quarantinable disease incident at an international airport, tasks that might be performed within the scope of each objective are to:

- Assist the Public
    - Provide mental health services for quarantine residents and support staff.
    - Address issues related to lost work and personal time.
    - Re-book flights.
- Restore the Environment
    - Decontaminate the airplane, the quarantine site(s), and transportation conveyances used to transport ill or exposed people.
    - Dispose of medical waste per established protocols.
- Restore the Infrastructure
- Establish systems for tracking and reporting on resources.
- Document resources committed to incident response.
- Maintain records of equipment and materials.
- Track personnel, equipment, and supplies.
- Maintain inventories of supplies.
- Replenish resources (i.e., medical supplies).
- Maintain accountability of expenditures.
- Maintain records of expenditures.

SECTION 9: AIRPORT COMMUNICABLE DISEASE RESPONSE PLANNING[1]

Introduction

The previous eight sections outline the "big picture" of the response to a quarantinable disease incident at an international airport. This section looks at planning for such an incident, more specifically, developing an international airport communicable disease response plan. In keeping with the big picture scope of the Manual, the planning template or guidance provided herein is not all inclusive nor does it go into detail. Mainly, it outlines the topics that might be covered in a communicable disease response plan and leaves it up to a planner to provide the specifics.

Contents of an Airport Communicable Disease Response Plan

Because the arrival of a quarantinable disease at an international airport may become an Incident of National Significance, elements and concepts of the NRP may apply to the response to and recovery from the event. Additionally, Homeland Security Presidential Directive 5 (HSPD5, February 28, 2003), regarding the management of domestic incidents, requires the use of the NIMS for all disaster responses. Therefore, airports should consider adopting the framework and terminology of the NRP and NIMS in their own airport communicable disease response plan. This framework and terminology is provided below. (For more information on the NRP, see http://www.dhs.gov/ dhspublic/interapp/editorial/editorial 0566.xml).

Introduction

The *Introduction* to the airport communicable disease response plan sets forth the *Purpose* and the *Scope and Applicability* of the plan. As the name implies, the *Purpose* contains the stated purpose for the plan. The *Scope and Applicability* subsection identifies what the plan covers and to whom it applies (i.e., what agencies and organizations).

---

[1] Note: When the word "airport" is used below, it refers to international airports, although this section on response planning could apply to and be used by domestic airports. Also, the use of the term "communicable disease response plan" refers to communicable diseases that are quarantinable, although airports may wish to address other diseases in their response plans.

Planning Assumptions and Considerations

In this section of the airport communicable disease response plan, the *Planning Assumptions and Considerations* upon which the airport communicable disease response plan is based are outlined. Several examples of planning assumptions and considerations taken from the NRP are as follows:

> Incidents are typically managed at the lowest possible geographic, organizational, and jurisdictional level.
>
> Incident management activities will be initiated and conducted using the principles contained in the NIMS.
>
> The combined expertise and capabilities of government at all levels, the private sector and nongovernmental organizations, will be required to prevent, prepare for, respond to, and recover from Incidents of National Significance.

An example of a planning assumption from an international airport communicable disease response plan is as follows:

> Only through a concerted and coordinated effort by all responding agencies can the situation be contained, reducing or preventing unnecessary exposure to personnel in the terminal; preventing potentially contaminated/contagious passengers from entering the community at large; allowing public health the opportunity to begin its epidemiological investigation; and allowing state and/or federal law enforcement agencies the opportunity to begin their investigation into a possible terrorist event.

Roles and Responsibilities

As the name implies, the *Roles and Responsibilities* section of the airport communicable disease response plan outlines the roles and responsibilities of all agencies and organizations involved in the response to and recovery from the incident. Examples of a roles and responsibilities section can be found in Section 4 of this Manual. However, an individual airport communicable disease response plan would want to go into more detail by clearly and definitively identifying organizations and individuals by name and providing contact information.

Concept of Operations

This section outlines the incident management structure and protocols that will be set in place to manage the airport communicable disease incident. As with the *Roles and Responsibilities* section, an individual airport communicable disease response plan would want to clearly and definitively describe its concept of operations. Examples of a concept of operations can be found in Appendix H of this document in the flowchart entitled "Unified Command Flowchart Example."

Incident Management Actions

This section describes the actual response to an airport communicable disease incident. Within the NRP, incident management actions are divided into five areas: notification and assessment, activation, response, recovery, and mitigation. For the purpose of the airport communicable disease response plan, these five areas pertain to:

1. Notification and Assessment – Pre- and post-confirmation notification requirements for a communicable disease incident at an airport; also, assessment requirements and protocols for assessing the incident. (*Notification and Assessment* requirements are covered in Sections 5 and 6 of this Manual.)
2. Activation – Activation and deployment of the response and support agencies and organizations; activation and deployment of the ICS. (*Activation* is covered in Section 5 of this Manual.)
3. Response – The activities that occur (as a result of notification, assessment, and activation) to address the communicable disease incident at the airport. These activities may include isolation or hospitalization of ill people and quarantine of exposed travelers. As with all sections of the airport communicable disease response plan, the requirements of this subsection will be clearly defined. (*Response* activities are outlined in Sections 5, 6, and 7 of this Manual)
4. Recovery – Actions needed to be taken to help individuals, communities, and agencies return to normal following the incident. (*Recovery* activities are addressed in Section 8 of this Manual.)
5. Mitigation – Activities designed to reduce or eliminate risks to persons or property or to lessen the actual or potential effects or consequences of an incident. (It is beyond the scope of this Manual to address mitigation activities.)

Ongoing Plan Management and Maintenance

This section of the airport communicable disease response plan describes actions that will be taken to update the plan based on new statutory requirements and lessons learned from exercises or actual incidents.

Appendices

The appendices include clarifying information (e.g., glossary of terms), references (e.g., statutes), and other material deemed necessary for and pertinent to supporting the contents of the airport communicable disease response plan.

Important Considerations for an Airport Communicable Disease Response Plan

The above information provides a framework from which airport authorities are able to design their airport communicable disease response plan, but does not explicitly identify the requisite contents of the plan. The provision of this information is left to airport authorities and responders to determine based on the airport location and its organizational and community structure. However, some important considerations for planners when putting together their plan are identified below.

- Clearly identified lines of authority. At international airports, the response to a quarantinable disease incident will be led by several federal agencies. The roles and responsibilities of these agencies as well as their statutory authority to undertake these roles and responsibilities needs to be clearly defined and explained in the airport communicable disease response plan. Additionally, any legal authority conveyed to state or local response agencies by these lead federal agencies needs to be clearly defined.
- Agreed upon incident management structure. In conjunction with clearly identified lines of authority, a clearly defined and agreed upon incident management structure needs to be developed prior to an actual communicable disease incident at an airport. An effective and efficient response requires all parties to be “on the same page” at the same time. Pre-incident planning could lead to this desired response.

- Pre-determined location(s) and assets for quarantine. Each international flight carries hundreds of travelers. Quarantining just one flight will require a large space and numerous assets to support the quarantine. The quarantine may require more than one location: a short-term site while laboratory diagnostic testing is performed to determine what disease is present, and a long-term site once positive confirmation has been determined and quarantine has been ordered. Both sites may be on or off the airport property. For the sake of the safety and the well-being of travelers, the airport itself, and the general public, it is imperative that planners determine ahead of time the location(s) and assets necessary to manage a large-scale, temporary quarantine or an extended quarantine.
- Management of public information. Today's world is one of fast and easily accessible and transmittable information. As soon as travelers on a plane suspect that a serious incident is occurring on their plane, they can be expected to use their cell phones to alert family, friends, and the media. Airport planners need to take a serious look at how they will handle the onslaught of media inquiries and reports from the very outset of the communicable disease incident. Airport public relations staff should consider developing contacts with their CDC counterparts before an incident occurs. Remember the old adage, "You only get one chance to make a good first impression."

APPENDIX A: CDC QUARANTINE STATIONS

Introduction

In response to concerns about disease importation and bioterrorism, DGMQ increased the number of stations and enhanced the training and response capability of its staff. Existing CDC Quarantine Stations were improved, and the number of Quarantine Stations increased to 18 in FY 2005, with more to be added in FY 2006. These field stations will provide advanced emergency response capabilities, including isolation and communications facilities. Regional health officers assigned to each station will provide clinical, epidemiologic, and programmatic support, and quarantine public health officers will conduct surveillance and response and communicable disease prevention activities. The transformed CDC Quarantine Stations will bring new expertise to bridge gaps in public health and clinical practice, emergency services, and response management.

Quarantine Station Listing

1. CDC Anchorage Quarantine Station
4600 Postmark Drive, Suite NC 206
Anchorage, AK 99502
(907) 271-6301
(907) 271-6325 (Fax)
Hours: Monday–Friday, 8:00 a.m.–4:30 p.m.
Jurisdiction: All ports in Alaska.

2. CDC Atlanta Quarantine Station
Hartsfield International Airport
P.O. Box 45256
Atlanta, GA 30320
(404) 639-1220
(404) 639-1224 (Fax)
Hours: Monday–Friday, 8:30 a.m.–6:30 p.m.
Jurisdiction: All ports in Georgia, Alabama, Arkansas, Louisiana, Mississippi, North Carolina, South Carolina, and Tennessee.

3. CDC Boston Quarantine Station
Terminal E
Logan International Airport
East Boston, MA 02128
(617) 820-6877 (Temporary)
(617) 561-5701
(617) 561-5708 (Fax)
Hours: Monday–Friday, 8:00 a.m.–4:30 p.m.
Jurisdiction: All ports in Massachusetts, Maine, New Hampshire, and Rhode Island.

4. CDC Chicago Quarantine Station
O'Hare International Airport
AMF O'Hare, POB 66012

Chicago, IL 60666-0012
(773) 894-2960
(773) 894-2970 (Fax)
Hours: Monday–Friday, 8:00 a.m.–8:00 p.m
Saturday, Sunday, and Holidays, 12:00 p.m.–8:00 p.m.
Jurisdiction: All ports in Illinois, Indiana, Iowa, Kansas, Missouri, and Wisconsin.
Canadian pre-clearance port: Toronto.

5. CDC Detroit Quarantine Station
2613 World Gateway Place
McNamara Terminal, Building 830
Detroit, MI 48242
(734) 955-6197
(734) 955-7790 (Fax)
Hours: Monday–Friday, 8:00 a.m.–4:30 p.m.
Jurisdiction: All ports in Michigan, Kentucky, and Ohio.

6. CDC El Paso Quarantine Station
Center for Border Health Research
1100 N. Stanton, Suite 410
El Paso, TX 79902
(915) 577-0970 (Extension 12 or 20)
(915) 543-2829 (24-hour Answering Service)
(915) 541-1137 (Fax)
Hours: Monday–Friday, 8:00 a.m.–4:30 p.m.
Jurisdiction: All ports in West Texas and New Mexico, including the U.S.-Mexico border for those two states.

7. CDC Honolulu Quarantine Station
Honolulu International Airport
300 Rodgers Blvd., #67
Honolulu, HI 96819-1897
(808) 861-8530
(808) 861-8532 (Fax)
Hours: Monday–Friday, 6:00 a.m.–4:00 p.m.
Jurisdiction: All ports in Hawaii, Guam, and Pacific Trust Territories.

8. CDC Houston Quarantine Station
George Bush Intercontinental Airport (IAH)
3870 North Terminal Road
C/O CBP, International Arrivals
U.S. Public Health Service, IA2.0833
Houston, Texas 77032
(281) 230-3784
Hours: Monday–Friday, 8:00 a.m.–5:30 p.m.
Jurisdiction: All ports in East Texas
(includes Dallas-Ft. Worth, Austin, and San Antonio),
Texas Gulf ports, and Oklahoma.

9. CDC Los Angeles Quarantine Station
Tom Bradley International Airport
380 World Way, Box N19
Los Angeles, CA 90045
(310) 215-2365
(310) 215-2285 (Fax)
Hours: Monday–Friday, 7:00 a.m.–4:30 p.m.
Saturday, Sunday, and Holidays, 8:00 a.m.–4:30 p.m.
Jurisdiction: All ports in Southern California, Nevada, and Arizona (excluding the U.S.-Mexico border). Southern California counties include Los Angeles, Orange, San Bernardino, Riverside, Ventura, Santa Barbara, and San Luis Obispo.

10. CDC Miami Quarantine Station
Miami International Airport
P.O. Box 996488
Miami, FL 33299-6488
(305) 526-2910
(305) 526-2798 (Fax)
Hours: Monday–Friday, 6:00 a.m.–4:00 p.m.
Saturday, Sunday, and Holidays, 8:00 a.m.–4:00 p.m.
Jurisdiction: All ports in Florida; Also, pre-clearance ports in the Bahamas.

11. CDC Minneapolis Quarantine Station
Minneapolis–St. Paul International Airport
Lindberg Terminal, Suite G-2256

4300 Glumack Drive
St. Paul, MN 55111
(612) 725-3005
Hours: Monday–Friday, 8:00 a.m.–4:30 p.m.
Jurisdiction: All ports in Minnesota, Nebraska, North Dakota, and South Dakota.

12. CDC Newark Quarantine Station
Newark Liberty International Airport
Terminal B - Box 52
Newark, NJ 07114
(973) 368-6200 (6201, 6202, and 6203)
(973) 368-6204 (Fax)
Hours: Monday–Friday, 9:00 a.m.–5:30 p.m.
Jurisdiction: All ports in New Jersey and Delaware.

13. CDC New York Quarantine Station
JFK International Airport
Room 219.016 Terminal 4 (E)
Jamaica, NY 11430-1081
(718) 553-1685
(718) 553-1524 (Fax)
Hours: Monday–Friday, 8:00 a.m.– 6:00 p.m.
Saturday, Sunday, and Holidays, 10:00 a.m.–6:00 p.m.
Jurisdiction: All ports in New York, Connecticut, Pennsylvania, and Vermont. Canadian pre-clearance port: Montreal. Also, pre-clearance ports at Bermuda, Shannon, and Dublin.

14. CDC San Diego Quarantine Station
CDC San Diego Quarantine Station
3851 Rosecrans St.
P.O. Box 85524, MS-P511B OBH
San Diego, CA 92138-5524
(619) 692-5659
(619) 692-8821 (Fax)
Hours: Monday–Friday, 8:00 a.m.–4:30 p.m.
Jurisdiction: All ports in San Diego and Imperial Counties of Southern California, and the U.S.-Mexico border crossings in California and Arizona.

15. CDC San Francisco Quarantine Station

San Francisco International Airport
PO Box 280548 SFIA
San Francisco, CA 94128-0548
(650) 876-2872
(650) 876-2796 (Fax)
Hours: Monday–Friday, 8:00 a.m.–4:30 p.m.
Jurisdiction: All ports in Central and Northern California (46 counties).

16. CDC San Juan Quarantine Station

CDC San Juan Quarantine Station
P.O. Box 37197
San Juan, PR 00937-0197
(787) 253-7868
(787) 774-7812 (Alternate phone)
Hours: Monday–Friday, 8:00 a.m.–4:30 p.m.
Jurisdiction: All ports in Puerto Rico and the U.S. Virgin Islands.

17. CDC Seattle Quarantine Station

Seattle-Tacoma International Airport, Room S-2067
Seattle, WA 98158-1250
(206) 553-4519
(206) 553-4455 (Fax)
Hours: Monday–Friday, 8:00 a.m.–4:30 p.m.

Jurisdiction: All ports in Washington, Colorado, Idaho, Montana, Oregon, Utah, and Wyoming. Canadian pre-clearance ports: Edmonton, Calgary, Vancouver, and Victoria.

18. CDC Washington Quarantine Station

Dulles International Airport
P.O. Box 17087
Washington, DC 20041
(703) 661-1320
(703) 661-1318 (Fax)
Hours: Monday–Friday, 8:00 a.m.–4:30 p.m.

Jurisdiction: All ports in Washington, DC, Maryland, Virginia, and West Virginia

New Quarantine Stations to be Added in 2006

19. CDC Dallas Quarantine Station
20. CDC Philadelphia Quarantine Station

APPENDIX B: TRAVEL NOTICES

Introduction

(From http://www.cdc.gov/travel/outbreaks.htm)

CDC issues different types of notices for international travelers. As of May 20, 2004, these definitions have been refined to make the announcements more easily understood by travelers, healthcare providers, and the general public. The definitions are laid out below. They describe both levels of risk for the traveler and recommended preventive measures to take at each level of risk.

Travel Notices: Interim Definitions and Criteria As of May 20, 2004

Rationale

CDC issues different types of notices for international travelers. We are refining these definitions to make the announcements more easily understood by travelers, healthcare providers, and the general public. In addition, defining and describing levels of risk for the traveler will clarify the need for the recommended preventive measures. From the public health perspective, scalable definitions will enhance the usefulness of the travel notices, enabling them to be tailored readily in response to events and circumstances.

1. **In the News:** notification by CDC of an occurrence of a disease of public health significance affecting a traveler or travel destination. The purpose is to provide information to travelers, Americans living abroad, and their healthcare providers about the disease. The risk for disease exposure is not thought to be increased beyond the usual baseline risk for that area, and only standard guidelines are recommended.

Type of Notice/Level of Concern	Scope*	Risk for Travelers†	Preventive Measures	Example of Notice	Example of Recommended Measures
In the News	Reports of sporadic cases	No increased risk over baseline for travelers observing standard recommendations	Keeping travelers informed and reinforcing standard prevention recommendations	Report of cases of dengue in Mexico, 2001	Reinforced standard recommendations for protection against insect bites
Outbreak Notice	Outbreak in limited geographic area or setting	Increased but definable and limited to specific settings	Reminders about standard and enhanced recommendations for the region	Outbreak of yellow fever in a state in Brazil in 2003	Reinforced enhanced recommendations, such as vaccination
Travel Health Precaution	Outbreak of greater scope affecting a larger geographic area	Increased in some settings, along with risk for spread to other areas	Specific precautions to reduce risk during the stay, and what to do before and after travel‡	Outbreak of avian influenza among poultry and humans in several countries in Southeast Asia in early 2004	Recommended specific precautions including avoiding areas with live poultry, such as live animal markets and poultry farms; ensuring poultry and eggs are thoroughly cooked; monitoring health
Travel Health Warning	Evidence that outbreak is expanding outside the area or populations initially affected	Increased because of evidence of transmission outside defined settings and/or inadequate containment measures	In addition to the specific precautions cited above, postpone nonessential travel‡	SARS outbreak in Asia in 2003	Recommended travelers to postpone nonessential travel because of level of risk

* The term "scope" incorporates the size, magnitude, and rapidity of spread of an outbreak.

† Risk for travelers is dependent on patterns of transmission, as well as severity of illness.

‡ Preventive measures other than the standard advice for the region may be recommended depending on the circumstances (e.g., travelers may be requested to monitor their health for a certain period after their return, or arriving passengers may be screened at ports of entry).

2. **Outbreak Notice:** notification by CDC that an outbreak of a disease is occurring in a limited geographic area or setting. The purpose of an outbreak notice is to provide accurate information to travelers and resident expatriates about the status of the outbreak and to remind travelers about the standard or enhanced travel recommendations for the area. Because of the limited nature of the outbreak, the risk for disease exposure is thought to be increased but defined and limited to specific settings.
3. **Travel Health Precaution:** ***CDC does NOT recommend against travel to the area.*** A travel health precaution is notification by CDC that a disease outbreak of greater scope is occurring in a more widespread geographic area. The purpose of a travel health precaution is to provide accurate information to travelers and Americans living abroad about the status of the outbreak (e.g., magnitude, scope, and rapidity of spread), specific precautions to reduce their risk for infection, and what to do if they become ill while in the area. The risk for the individual traveler is thought to be increased in defined settings or associated with specific risk factors (e.g., transmission in a healthcare or hospital setting where ill patients are being cared for).
4. **Travel Health Warning:** ***CDC recommends against nonessential travel to the area.*** A travel health warning is a notification by CDC that a widespread, serious outbreak of a disease of public health concern is expanding outside the area or populations that were initially affected. The purpose of a travel health warning is to provide accurate information to travelers and Americans living abroad about the status of the outbreak (e.g., its scope, magnitude, and rapidity of spread), how they can reduce their risk for infection, and what to do if they should become ill while in the area. The warning also serves to reduce the volume of traffic to the affected areas, which in turn can reduce the risk of spreading the disease to previously unaffected sites. **CDC recommends against nonessential travel to the area** because the risk for the traveler is considered to be high (i.e., the risk is increased because of evidence of transmission outside defined settings or inadequate containment). Additional preventive measures may be recommended, depending on the circumstances (e.g., travelers may be requested to monitor their health for a certain period after their return; arriving passengers may be screened at ports of entry).

Criteria for Instituting Travel Notices

- Disease transmission: The modes of transmission and patterns of spread, as well as the magnitude and scope of the outbreak in the area, will affect the decision for the appropriate level of notice. Criteria include the presence or absence of transmission outside defined settings, as well as evidence that cases have spread to other areas.
- Containment measures: The presence or absence of acceptable outbreak control measures in the affected area can influence the decision for what level of notice to issue. Areas where the disease is occurring that are considered to have poor or no containment measures in place have the potential for a higher risk of transmission to exposed persons and spread to other areas.
- Quality of surveillance: Criteria include whether health authorities in the area have the ability to accurately detect and report cases and conduct appropriate contact tracing of exposed persons. Areas where the disease is occurring that are considered to have poor surveillance systems may have the potential for a higher risk of transmission.
- Quality and accessibility of medical care: Areas where the disease is occurring that are considered to have inadequate medical services and infection control procedures in place, as well as remote locations without access to medical evacuation, present a higher level of risk for the traveler or Americans living abroad.

Criteria for Downgrading or Removing Notices

To downgrade a travel health warning to a travel health precaution, there should be:

- Adequate and regularly updated reports of surveillance data from the area
- No evidence of ongoing transmission outside defined settings for two incubation periods after the date of onset of symptoms for the last case, as reported by public health officials.
- To remove a **travel precaution**, there should be:
- Adequate and regularly updated reports of surveillance data from the area
- No evidence of new cases for three incubation periods after the date of onset of symptoms for the last case, as reported by public health authorities.

- Limited or no recent instances of exported cases from the area; this criterion excludes intentional or planned evacuations.

In the News and Outbreak Notices will be revisited at regular intervals and will be removed when no longer relevant or when the outbreak has resolved.

APPENDIX C: PERSONAL PROTECTIVE EQUIPMENT (PPE)

Note

It is beyond the scope of this Manual to provide detailed information about the various types of PPE as well as detailed instructions on its proper use. As has been pointed out earlier in the Manual, those providing and donning surgical masks or respiratory protection should be trained in the proper types and appropriate uses of this PPE. Therefore, a certified professional should be consulted when selecting PPE and training responders on its proper use.

As has also been pointed out earlier, fairly simple infection control practices can help to minimize the transmission of respiratory disease. For example, placing a surgical mask on ill person(s), if the person can tolerate wearing one is very important. If they cannot wear a surgical mask they should be instructed to practice respiratory/cough etiquette (see the following CDC web site at: www.cdc.gov/flu/professionals/infectioncontrol/resphygiene.htm). In addition, transmission can be reduced through the use of good hand hygiene.

Resources

In addition to the above mentioned web site, there are several good web sites that provide more information on the proper use of PPE. These are listed below.

1. Centers for Disease Control and Prevention, Smallpox Response Plan and Guidelines Infection Control Measures for Healthcare and Community Settings, Available at http://www.bt.cdc.gov/agent/smallpox/response-plan/files/guide-c-part-1.pdf.

2. Centers for Disease Control and Prevention, Guideline for Isolation Precautions in Hospitals, Available at http://www.cdc.gov/ncidod/dhqp/gl isolation ptII.html.
3. Centers for Disease Control and Prevention, Supplement I: Infection Control in Healthcare, Home, and Community Settings, Infection Control for Prehospital Emergency Medical Services, Available at http://www.cdc.gov/ncidod/sars/guidance/I/word/prehospital.doc .
4. Occupational Safety and Health Administration-Safety and Health Topics- Respiratory Protection, Available at http://www.osha.gov/SLTC/respiratoryprotection/index.html
5. Occupational Safety and Health Administration-Respiratory Protection E-tool, Available at http://www.osha.gov/SLTC/etools/respiratory/index.html.
6. NIOSH-Respirator Decision Logic-http://www.trustcrm.com/ectny/respiratory advisor/oshafiles/appendixe.html.

APPENDIX D: FACT SHEET: LEGAL AUTHORITIES FOR ISOLATION AND QUARANTINE

[From: http://www.cdc.gov/ncidod/dq/factsheetlegal.htm (Updated February 24, 2006)]

Introduction

- **Isolation** and **quarantine** are two common public health strategies designed to protect the public by preventing exposure to infected or potentially infected persons.
- In general, **isolation** refers to the separation of persons who have a specific infectious illness from those who are healthy and the restriction of their movement to stop the spread of that illness. Isolation is a standard procedure used in hospitals today for patients with tuberculosis and certain other infectious diseases.
- **Quarantine**, in contrast, generally refers to the separation and restriction of movement of persons who, while not yet ill, have been exposed to an infectious agent and therefore may become infectious.

Quarantine of exposed persons is a public health strategy, like isolation, that is intended to stop the spread of infectious disease.

- Both isolation and quarantine may be conducted on a **voluntary basis** or **compelled on a mandatory basis** through legal authority.

State/Local and Tribal Law

- A state's authority to compel isolation and quarantine within its borders is derived from its inherent "police power"—the authority of a state government to enact laws and promote regulations to safeguard the health, safety, and welfare of its citizens. As a result of this authority, the individual states are responsible for intrastate isolation and quarantine practices, and they conduct their activities in accordance with their respective statutes.
- Tribal laws and regulations are similar in promoting the health, safety, and welfare of tribal members. Tribal health authorities are responsible for isolation and quarantine practices within tribal lands in accordance with their respective laws.
- State and local laws and regulations regarding the issues of compelled isolation and quarantine vary widely. Historically, some states have codified extensive procedural provisions related to the enforcement of these public health measures, whereas other states rely on older statutory provisions that can be very broad. In some jurisdictions, local health departments are governed by the provisions of state law; in other settings, local health authorities may be responsible for enforcing state or more stringent local measures. In many states, violation of a quarantine order constitutes a criminal misdemeanor.
- Examples of other public health actions that can be compelled by legal authorities include disease reporting, immunization for school attendance, and tuberculosis treatment.

Federal Law

- The HHS Secretary has statutory responsibility for preventing the introduction, transmission, and spread of communicable diseases from foreign countries into the United States, e.g., at international ports of arrival, and from one state or possession into another.

- The communicable diseases for which federal isolation and quarantine are authorized are set forth through executive order of the President and include **cholera**, **diphtheria**, **infectious tuberculosis**, **plague**, **smallpox**, **yellow fever**, **viral hemorrhagic fevers**, and **severe acute respiratory syndrome (SARS)**. In April 2005, the President added to this list **Influenza caused by novel or reemergent influenza viruses that are causing, or have the potential to cause, a pandemic**.
- By statute, CBP and Coast Guard officers are required to aid in the enforcement of quarantine rules and regulations. Violation of federal quarantine rules and regulations constitutes a criminal misdemeanor, punishable by fine and imprisonment.
- Federal quarantine authority includes the authority to release persons from quarantine on the condition that they comply with medical monitoring and surveillance.

Interplay between Federal and State/Local Laws

- States and local jurisdictions have primary responsibility for isolation and quarantine within their borders. The federal government has authority under the Commerce Clause of the U.S. Constitution to prevent the interstate spread of disease.
- The federal government has primary responsibility for preventing the introduction of communicable diseases from foreign countries into the United States.
- By statute, the HHS Secretary may accept state and local assistance in the enforcement of federal quarantine regulations and may assist state and local officials in the control of communicable diseases.
- It is possible for federal, state, and local health authorities simultaneously to have separate but concurrent legal quarantine power in a particular situation (e.g., an arriving aircraft at a large city airport).
- Because isolation and quarantine are "police power" functions, public health officials at the federal, state, and local levels may occasionally seek the assistance of their respective law enforcement counterparts to enforce a public health order.

Appendix E: Executive Orders on Quarantinable Diseases

Executive Order 13295 of April 4, 2003

Revised List of Quarantinable Communicable Diseases

By the authority vested in me as President by the Constitution and the laws of the United States of America, including section 361(b) of the Public Health Service Act (42 U.S.C. 264(b)), it is hereby ordered as follows:

Section 1. Based upon the recommendation of the Secretary of Health and Human Services (the ``Secretary"), in consultation with the Surgeon General, and for the purpose of specifying certain communicable diseases for regulations providing for the apprehension, detention, or conditional release of individuals to prevent the introduction, transmission, or spread of suspected communicable diseases, the following communicable diseases are hereby specified pursuant to section 361(b) of the Public Health Service Act:

a) Cholera; Diphtheria; infectious Tuberculosis; Plague; Smallpox; Yellow Fever; and Viral Hemorrhagic Fevers (Lassa, Marburg, Ebola, Crimean-Congo, South American, and others not yet isolated or named).
b) Severe Acute Respiratory Syndrome (SARS), which is a disease associated with fever and signs and symptoms of pneumonia or other respiratory illness, is transmitted from person to person predominantly by the aerosolized or droplet route, and, if spread in the population, would have severe public health consequences.

Sec. 2. The Secretary, in the Secretary's discretion, shall determine whether a particular condition constitutes a communicable disease of the type specified in section 1 of this order.

Sec. 3. The functions of the President under sections 362 and 364(a) of the Public Health Service Act (42 U.S.C. 265 and 267(a)) are assigned to the Secretary.

Sec. 4. This order is not intended to, and does not, create any right or benefit enforceable at law or equity by any party against the United States, its departments, agencies, entities, officers, employees or agents, or any other person.

Sec. 5. Executive Order 12452 of December 22, 1983, is hereby revoked. George W. Bush

THE WHITE HOUSE,
April 4, 2003.

For Immediate Release
Office of the Press Secretary
April 1, 2005

Executive Order: Amendment to E.O. 13295 Relating to Certain Influenza Viruses and Quarantinable Communicable Diseases

By the authority vested in me as President by the Constitution and the laws of the United States of America, including section 361(b) of the Public Health Service Act (42 U.S.C. 264(b)), it is hereby ordered as follows:

Section 1. Based upon the recommendation of the Secretary of Health and Human Services, in consultation with the Surgeon General, and for the purpose set forth in section 1 of Executive Order 13295 of April 4, 2003, section 1 of such order is amended by adding at the end thereof the following new subsection:

"(c) Influenza caused by novel or reemergent influenza viruses that are causing, or have the potential to cause, a pandemic.".

Sec. 2. This order is not intended to, and does not, create any right or benefit, substantive or procedural, enforceable at law or in equity by any party against the United States, its departments, agencies, entities, officers, employees or agents, or any other person.

GEORGE W. BUSH
THE WHITE HOUSE,
April 1, 2005.

Appendix F: Quarantinable Disease Information

Cholera

(From http://www.cdc.gov/ncidod/dbmd/diseaseinfo/cholera g.htm)

Disease History

In January 1991, epidemic cholera appeared in South America and quickly spread to several countries. A few cases have occurred in the United States among persons who traveled to South America or ate contaminated food brought back by travelers.

Cholera has been very rare in industrialized nations for the last 100 years; however, the disease is still common today in other parts of the world, including the Indian subcontinent and sub-Saharan Africa.

Although cholera can be life-threatening, it is easily prevented and treated. In the United States, because of advanced water and sanitation systems, cholera is not a major threat; however, everyone, especially travelers, should be aware of how the disease is transmitted and what can be done to prevent it.

What Is Cholera?

Cholera is an acute, diarrheal illness caused by infection of the intestine with the bacterium *Vibrio cholerae*. The infection is often mild or without symptoms, but sometimes it can be severe. Approximately one in 20 infected persons has severe disease characterized by profuse watery diarrhea, vomiting, and leg cramps. In these persons, rapid loss of body fluids leads to dehydration and shock. Without treatment, death can occur within hours.

How Does a Person Get Cholera?

A person may get cholera by drinking water or eating food contaminated with the cholera bacterium. In an epidemic, the source of the contamination is usually the feces of an infected person. The disease can spread rapidly in areas with inadequate treatment of sewage and drinking water.

The cholera bacterium may also live in the environment in brackish rivers and coastal waters. Shellfish eaten raw have been a source of cholera, and a few persons in the United States have contracted cholera after eating raw or undercooked shellfish from the Gulf of Mexico. The disease is not likely to spread directly from one person to another; therefore, casual contact with an infected person is not a risk for becoming ill.

What Is the Risk for Cholera in the United States?

In the United States, cholera was prevalent in the 1800s but has been virtually eliminated by modern sewage and water treatment systems. However, as a result of improved transportation, more persons from the United States travel to parts of Africa, Asia, or Latin America where epidemic cholera is occurring. U.S. travelers to areas with epidemic cholera may be exposed to the cholera bacterium. In addition, travelers may bring contaminated seafood back to the United States; foodborne outbreaks have been caused by contaminated seafood brought into this country by travelers.

What Should Travelers Do to Avoid Getting Cholera?

The risk for cholera is very low for U.S. travelers visiting areas with epidemic cholera. When simple precautions are observed, contracting the disease is unlikely.

All travelers to areas where cholera has occurred should observe the following recommendations:

- Drink only water that you have boiled or treated with chlorine or iodine. Other safe beverages include tea and coffee made with boiled water and carbonated, bottled beverages with no ice.
- Eat only foods that have been thoroughly cooked and are still hot, or fruit that you have peeled yourself.
- Avoid undercooked or raw fish or shellfish, including ceviche.
- Make sure all vegetables are cooked avoid salads.
- Avoid foods and beverages from street vendors.
- Do not bring perishable seafood back to the United States.
- A simple rule of thumb is "Boil it, cook it, peel it, or forget it."

Is a Vaccine Available to Prevent Cholera?

At the present time, the manufacture and sale of the only licensed cholera vaccine in the United States (Wyeth-Ayerst) has been discontinued. It has not been recommended for travelers because of the brief and incomplete immunity it offers. No cholera vaccination requirements exist for entry or exit in any country.

Two recently developed vaccines for cholera are licensed and available in other countries (Dukoral®, Biotec AB and Mutacol®, Berna). Both vaccines appear to provide a somewhat better immunity and fewer side-effects than the previously available vaccine. However, neither of these two vaccines is recommended for travelers nor are they available in the United States.

Can Cholera Be Treated?

Cholera can be simply and successfully treated by immediate replacement of the fluid and salts lost through diarrhea. Patients can be treated with oral rehydration solution, a prepackaged mixture of sugar and salts to be mixed with water and drunk in large amounts. This solution is used throughout the world to treat diarrhea. Severe cases also require intravenous fluid replacement. With prompt rehydration, fewer than 1% of cholera patients die.

Antibiotics shorten the course and diminish the severity of the illness, but they are not as important as rehydration. Persons who develop severe diarrhea and vomiting in countries where cholera occurs should seek medical attention promptly.

What Is the U.S. Government Doing to Combat Cholera?

U.S. and international public health authorities are working to enhance surveillance for cholera, investigate cholera outbreaks, and design and implement preventive measures. The Centers for Disease Control and Prevention investigates epidemic cholera wherever it occurs and trains laboratory workers in proper techniques for identification of *V. cholerae*. In addition, the Centers for Disease Control and Prevention provides information on diagnosis, treatment, and prevention of cholera to public health officials and educates the public about effective preventive measures.

The U.S. Agency for International Development is sponsoring some of the international government activities and is providing medical supplies to affected countries.

The Environmental Protection Agency is working with water and sewage treatment operators in the United States to prevent contamination of water with the cholera bacterium.

The Food and Drug Administration is testing imported and domestic shellfish for *V. cholerae* and monitoring the safety of U.S. shellfish beds through the shellfish sanitation program.

With cooperation at the state and local, national, and international levels, assistance will be provided to countries where cholera is present, and the risk to U.S. residents will remain small.

Diphtheria

(From http://www.cdc.gov/ncidod/dbmd/diseaseinfo/diptheria t.htm)

Clinical Features

Respiratory diphtheria presents as a sore throat with low-grade fever and an adherent membrane of the tonsils, pharynx, or nose. Neck swelling is usually present in severe disease. Cutaneous diphtheria presents as infected skin lesions which lack a characteristic appearance.

Etiologic Agent

Toxin-producing strains of Corynebacterium diphtheriae.

Incidence

Approximately 0.001 cases per 100,000 population in the U.S. since 1980; before the introduction of vaccine in the 1920s incidence was 100-200 cases per 100,000 population. Diphtheria remains endemic in developing countries. The countries of the former Soviet Union have reported >150,000 cases in an epidemic which began in 1990.

Complications

Myocarditis (inflammation of the heart muscle), polyneuritis (inflammation of several peripheral nerves at the same time), and airway obstruction are common complications of respiratory diphtheria; death occurs in 5%-10% of respiratory cases. Complications and deaths are much less frequent in cutaneous diphtheria.

Transmission

Direct person-to-person transmission by intimate respiratory and physical contact. Cutaneous lesions are important in transmission.

Risk Groups

In the pre-vaccine era, children were at highest risk for respiratory diphtheria. Recently, diphtheria has primarily affected adults in the sporadic cases reported in the U.S. and in the large outbreaks in Russia and New Independent States of the Former Soviet Union.

Challenges

Circulation appears to continue in some settings even in populations with >80% childhood immunization rates. An asymptomatic carrier state exists even among immune individuals. Immunity wanes over time; decennial booster doses are required to maintain protective antibody levels. Large populations of adults are susceptible to diphtheria in developed countries—appear to be increasing in developing countries as well.

In countries with low incidence, the diagnosis may not be considered by clinician and laboratory scientists. Prior antibiotic treatment can prevent recovery of the organism.

Limited epidemiologic, clinical and laboratory expertise on diphtheria.

Infectious Tuberculosis

(From http://www.cdc.gov/nchstp/tb/faqs/qa.htm)

What Is TB?

Tuberculosis (TB) is a disease caused by bacteria called *Mycobacterium tuberculosis*. The bacteria usually attack the lungs. But, TB bacteria can attack any part of the body such as the kidney, spine, and brain. If not treated properly, TB disease can be fatal. TB disease was once the leading cause of death in the United States.

TB is spread through the air from one person to another. The bacteria are put into the air when a person with active TB disease of the lungs or throat coughs or sneezes. People nearby may breathe in these bacteria and become infected.

However, not everyone infected with TB bacteria becomes sick. People who are not sick have what is called latent TB infection. People who have latent TB infection do not feel sick, do not have any symptoms, and cannot spread TB to others. But, some people with latent TB infection go on to get TB disease.

People with active TB disease can be treated and cured if they seek medical help. Even better, people with latent TB infection can take medicine so that they will not develop active TB disease.

Why Is TB A Problem Today?

Starting in the 1940s, scientists discovered the first of several medicines now used to treat TB. As a result, TB slowly began to decrease in the United States. But in the 1970s and early 1980s, the country let its guard down and TB control efforts were neglected. As a result, between 1985 and 1992, the number of TB cases increased. However, with increased funding and attention to the TB problem, we have had a steady decline in the number of persons with TB since 1992. But TB is still a problem; more than 14,000 cases were reported in 2003 in the United States.

This booklet answers common questions about TB. Please ask your doctor or nurse if you have other questions about latent TB infection or TB disease.

How Is TB Spread?

TB is spread through the air from one person to another. The bacteria are put into the air when a person with active TB disease of the lungs or throat coughs or sneezes. People nearby may breathe in these bacteria and become infected.

When a person breathes in TB bacteria, the bacteria can settle in the lungs and begin to grow. From there, they can move through the blood to other parts of the body, such as the kidney, spine, and brain.

TB in the lungs or throat can be infectious. This means that the bacteria can be spread to other people. TB in other parts of the body, such as the kidney or spine, is usually not infectious. People with active TB disease are most likely to spread it to people they spend time with every day. This includes family members, friends, and coworkers.

What Is Latent TB Infection?

In most people who breathe in TB bacteria and become infected, the body is able to fight the bacteria to stop them from growing. The bacteria become inactive, but they remain alive in the body and can become active later. This is called latent TB infection. People with latent TB infection:

- Have no symptoms.
- Don't feel sick.
- Can't spread TB to others.
- Usually have a positive skin test reaction.
- Can develop active TB disease if they do not receive treatment for latent TB infection.

Many people who have latent TB infection never develop active TB disease. In these people, the TB bacteria remain inactive for a lifetime without causing disease. But in other people, especially people who have weak immune systems, the bacteria become active and cause TB disease.

What Is Active TB Disease?

TB bacteria become active if the immune system can't stop them from growing. The active bacteria begin to multiply in the body and cause active TB disease. The bacteria attack the body and destroy tissue. If this occurs in the lungs, the bacteria can actually create a hole in the lung. Some people develop active TB disease soon after becoming infected, before their immune system can fight the TB bacteria. Other people may get sick later, when their immune system becomes weak for another reason.

Babies and young children often have weak immune systems. People infected with HIV, the virus that causes AIDS, have very weak immune systems. Other people can have weak immune systems, too, especially people with any of these conditions: substance abuse, diabetes mellitus, silicosis, cancer of the head or neck, leukemia or Hodgkin's disease, severe kidney disease, low body weight, certain medical treatments (such as corticosteroid treatment or organ transplants), and specialized treatment for rheumatoid arthritis or Crohn's disease.

Symptoms of TB depend on where in the body the TB bacteria are growing. TB bacteria usually grow in the lungs. TB in the lungs may cause symptoms such as:

- A bad cough that lasts 3 weeks or longer.
- Pain in the chest.
- Coughing up blood or sputum (phlegm from deep inside the lungs).

Other symptoms of active TB disease are:

- Weakness or fatigue
- Weight loss
- No appetite
- Chills
- Fever
- Sweating at night

Plague

(From http://www.cdc.gov/ncidod/dvbid/plague/info.htm)

General Information

Plague, caused by a bacterium called *Yersinia pestis*, is transmitted from rodent to rodent by infected fleas.

Plague is characterized by periodic disease outbreaks in rodent populations, some of which have a high death rate. During these outbreaks, hungry infected fleas that have lost their normal hosts seek other sources of blood, thus increasing the increased risk to humans and other animals frequenting the area.

Epidemics of plague in humans usually involve house rats and their fleas. Rat-borne epidemics continue to occur in some developing countries, particularly in rural areas. The last rat-borne epidemic in the United States occurred in Los Angeles in 1924-25. Since then, all human plague cases in the U.S. have been sporadic cases acquired from wild rodents or their fleas or from direct contact with plague-infected animals.

Rock squirrels and their fleas are the most frequent sources of human infection in the southwestern states. For the Pacific states, the California ground squirrel and its fleas are the most common source. Many other rodent species, for instance, prairie dogs, wood rats, chipmunks, and other ground squirrels and their fleas, suffer plague outbreaks and some of these occasionally serve as sources of human infection. Deer mice and voles are thought to maintain the disease in animal populations but are less important as sources of human infection. Other less frequent sources of infection include wild rabbits, and wild carnivores that pick up their infections from wild rodent outbreaks. Domestic cats (and sometimes dogs) are readily infected by fleas or from eating infected wild rodents. Cats may serve as a source of infection to persons exposed to them. Pets may also bring plague-infected fleas into the home.

Between outbreaks, the plague bacterium is believed to circulate within populations of certain species of rodents without causing excessive mortality. Such groups of infected animals serve as silent, long-term reservoirs of infection.

Geographic Distribution of Plague

In the United States during the 1980s plague cases averaged about 18 per year. Most of the cases occurred in persons under 20 years of age. About 1 in 7 persons with plague died.

Worldwide, there are 1,000 to 2,000 cases each year. During the 1980s epidemic plague occurred each year in Africa, Asia, or South America. Epidemic plague is generally associated with domestic rats. Almost all of the cases reported during the decade were rural and occurred among people living in small towns and villages or agricultural areas rather than in larger, more developed, towns and cities.

The following information provides a worldwide distribution pattern:

- There is no plague in Australia.
- There is no plague in Europe; the last reported cases occurred after World War II.
- In Asia and extreme southeastern Europe, plague is distributed from the Caucasus Mountains in Russia, through much of the Middle East, eastward through China, and hen southward to Southwest and Southeast Asia, where it occurs in scattered, localized foci. Within these plague foci, there are isolated human cases and occasional outbreaks. Plague regularly occurs in Madagascar, off the southeastern coast of Africa.
- In Africa, plague foci are distributed from Uganda south on the eastern side of the continent, and in southern Africa. Severe outbreaks have occurred in recent years in Kenya, Tanzania, Zaire, Mozambique, and Botswana, with smaller outbreaks in other East African countries. Plague also has been reported in scattered foci in western and northern Africa.
- In North America, plague is found from the Pacific Coast eastward to the western Great Plains and from British Columbia and Alberta, Canada southward to Mexico. Most of the human cases occur in two regions; one in northern New Mexico, northern Arizona, and southern Colorado, another in California, southern Oregon, and far western Nevada.
- In South America, active plague foci exist in two regions; the Andean mountain region (including parts of Bolivia, Peru, and Ecuador) and in Brazil.

How Is Plague Transmitted?

Plague is transmitted from animal to animal and from animal to human by the bites of infective fleas. Less frequently, the organism enters through a break in the skin by direct contact with tissue or body fluids of a plague-infected animal, for instance, in the process of skinning a rabbit or other animal. Plague is also transmitted by inhaling infected droplets expelled by coughing, by a person or animal, especially domestic cats, with pneumonic plague. Transmission of plague from person to person is uncommon and has not been observed in the United States since 1924 but does occur as an important factor in plague epidemics in some developing countries.

Diagnosis

The pathognomic sign of plague is a very painful, usually swollen, and often hot-to-the touch lymph node, called a bubo. This finding, accompanied with fever, extreme exhaustion, and a history of possible exposure to rodents, rodent fleas, wild rabbits, or sick or dead carnivores should lead to suspicion of plague.

Onset of bubonic plague is usually 2 to 6 days after a person is exposed. Initial manifestations include fever, headache, and general illness, followed by the development of painful, swollen regional lymph nodes. Occasionally, buboes cannot be detected for a day or so after the onset of other symptoms. The disease progresses rapidly and the bacteria can invade the bloodstream, producing severe illness, called plague septicemia.

Once a human is infected, a progressive and potentially fatal illness generally results unless specific antibiotic therapy is given. Progression leads to blood infection and, finally, to lung infection. The infection of the lung is termed *plague pneumonia*, and it can be transmitted to others through the expulsion of infective respiratory droplets by coughing.

The incubation period of primary pneumonic plague is 1 to 3 days and is characterized by development of an overwhelming pneumonia with high fever, cough, bloody sputum, and chills. For plague pneumonia patients, the death rate is over 50%.

Treatment Information

As soon as a diagnosis of suspected plague is made, the patient should be isolated, and local and state health departments should be notified. Confirmatory laboratory work should be initiated, including blood cultures and examination of lymph node specimens if possible. Drug therapy should begin as soon as possible after the laboratory specimens are taken. The drugs of choice are streptomycin or gentamycin, but a number of other antibiotics are also effective.

Those individuals closely associated with the patient, particularly in cases with pneumonia, should be traced, identified, and evaluated. Contacts of pneumonic plague patients should be placed under observation or given preventive antibiotic therapy, depending on the degree and timing of contact.

It is a U.S. Public Health Service requirement that all suspected plague cases be reported to local and state health departments and the diagnosis confirmed by CDC. As required by the International Health Regulations, CDC reports all U.S. plague cases to the World Health Organization.

Prevention

Plague will probably continue to exist in its many localized geographic areas around the world, and plague outbreaks in wild rodent hosts will continue to occur. Attempts to eliminate wild rodent plague are costly and futile. Therefore, primary preventive measures are directed toward reducing the threat of infection in humans in high risk areas through three techniques—environmental management, public health education, and preventive drug therapy.

Preventive Drug Therapy

Antibiotics may be taken in the event of exposure to the bites of wild rodent fleas during an outbreak or to the tissues or fluids of a plague-infected animal. Preventive therapy is also recommended in the event of close exposure to another person or to a pet animal with suspected plague pneumonia. For preventive drug therapy, the preferred antibiotics are the tetracyclines, chloramphenicol, or one of the effective sulfonamides.

Vaccines

The plague vaccine is no longer commercially available in the United States.

Smallpox

(From http://www.bt.cdc.gov/agent/smallpox/overview/disease-facts.asp)

The Disease

Smallpox is a serious, contagious, and sometimes fatal infectious disease. There is no specific treatment for smallpox disease, and the only prevention is vaccination. The name *smallpox* is derived from the Latin word for "spotted" and refers to the raised bumps that appear on the face and body of an infected person.

There are two clinical forms of smallpox. Variola major is the severe and most common form of smallpox, with a more extensive rash and higher fever. There are four types of variola major smallpox: ordinary (the most frequent type, accounting for 90% or more of cases); modified (mild and occurring in previously vaccinated persons); flat; and hemorrhagic (both rare and very severe). Historically, variola major has an overall fatality rate of about 30%; however, flat and hemorrhagic smallpox usually are fatal. Variola minor is a less common presentation of smallpox, and a much less severe disease, with death rates historically of 1% or less.

Smallpox outbreaks have occurred from time to time for thousands of years, but the disease is now eradicated after a successful worldwide vaccination program. The last case of smallpox in the United States was in 1949. The last naturally occurring case in the world was in Somalia in 1977. After the disease was eliminated from the world, routine vaccination against smallpox among the general public was stopped because it was no longer necessary for prevention.

Where Smallpox Comes From

Smallpox is caused by the variola virus that emerged in human populations thousands of years ago. Except for laboratory stockpiles, the variola virus has been eliminated. However, in the aftermath of the events of October and October, 2001, there is heightened concern that the variola virus might be used as an agent of bioterrorism. For this reason, the U.S. government is taking precautions for dealing with a smallpox outbreak.

Transmission

Generally, direct and fairly prolonged face-to-face contact is required to spread smallpox from one person to another. Smallpox also can be spread through direct contact with infected bodily fluids or contaminated objects such as bedding or clothing. Rarely, smallpox has been spread by virus carried in the air in enclosed settings such as buildings, buses, and trains. Humans are the only natural hosts of variola. Smallpox is not known to be transmitted by insects or animals.

A person with smallpox is sometimes contagious with onset of fever (prodrome phase), but the person becomes most contagious with the onset of rash. At this stage the infected person is usually very sick and not able to move around in the community. The infected person is contagious until the last smallpox scab falls off.

Smallpox Disease	
Incubation Period (Duration: 7 to 17 days) *Not contagious*	Exposure to the virus is followed by an incubation period during which people do not have any symptoms and may feel fine. This incubation period averages about 12 to 14 days but can range from 7 to 17 days. During this time, people are not contagious.

(Continued)

Initial Symptoms *(Prodrome)* (Duration: 2 to 4 days) *Sometimes contagious**	The first symptoms of smallpox include fever, malaise, head and body aches, and sometimes vomiting. The fever is usually high, in the range of 101 to 104 degrees Fahrenheit. At this time, people are usually too sick to carry on their normal activities. This is called the *prodrome* phase and may last for 2 to 4 days.
Early Rash (Duration: about 4 days) *Most contagious*	A rash emerges first as small red spots on the tongue and in the mouth. These spots develop into sores that break open and spread large amounts of the virus into the mouth and throat. At this time, the person becomes most contagious. Around the time the sores in the mouth break down, a rash appears on the skin, starting on the face and spreading to the arms and legs and then to the hands and feet. Usually the rash spreads to all parts of the body within 24 hours. As the rash appears, the fever usually falls and the person may start to feel better. By the third day of the rash, the rash becomes raised bumps. By the fourth day, the bumps fill with a thick, opaque fluid and often have a depression in the center that looks like a bellybutton. (This is a major distinguishing characteristic of smallpox.) Fever often will rise again at this time and remain high until scabs form over the bumps.
Pustular Rash (Duration: about 5 days) *Contagious*	The bumps become pustules—sharply raised, usually round and firm to the touch as if there's a small round object under the skin. People often say the bumps feel like BB pellets embedded in the skin.
Pustules and Scabs (Duration: about 5 days) *Contagious*	The pustules begin to form a crust and then scab. By the end of the second week after the rash appears, most of the sores have scabbed over.
Resolving Scabs (Duration: about 6 days) *Contagious*	The scabs begin to fall off, leaving marks on the skin that eventually become pitted scars. Most scabs will have fallen off three weeks after the rash appears. The person is contagious to others until all of the scabs have fallen off.
Scabs resolved *Not contagious*	Scabs have fallen off. Person is no longer contagious.

* Smallpox may be contagious during the *prodrome* phase, but is most infectious during the first 7 to 10 days following rash onset.

Yellow Fever

(From http://www.cdc.gov/ncidod/dvbid/yellowfever/index.htm)

Disease Information

Yellow fever occurs only in Africa and South America. In South America sporadic infections occur almost exclusively in forestry and agricultural workers from occupational exposure in or near forests.

In Africa the virus is transmitted in three geographic regions:

- Principally and foremost, in the moist savanna zones of West and Central Africa during the rainy season,
- Secondly, outbreaks occur occasionally in urban locations and villages in Africa, and
- Finally, to a lesser extent, in jungle regions.

Yellow fever is a viral disease transmitted between humans by a mosquito. Yellow fever is a very rare cause of illness in travelers, but most countries have regulations and requirements for yellow fever vaccination that must be met prior to entering the country. General precautions to avoid mosquito bites should be followed. These include the use of insect repellent, protective clothing, and mosquito netting. Yellow fever vaccine is a live virus vaccine which has been used for several decades. A single dose confers immunity lasting 10 years or more. If a person is at continued risk of yellow fever infection, a booster dose is needed every 10 years. Adults and children over 9 months can take this vaccine. Administration of immune globulin does not interfere with the antibody response to yellow fever vaccine.

This vaccine is only administered at designated yellow fever vaccination centers; the locations of which can usually be given by your local health department. Information regarding registered yellow fever vaccination sites can be viewed at the CDC Travelers' Health Yellow Fever website.

Note: Vaccination recommendations have recently changed (MMWR Nov. 8, 2002). In addition, there have been recent reports documenting patients between 1996 and 2001 who developed severe illness potentially related to yellow fever vaccination.

Who Should Not Receive the Yellow Fever Vaccine?

Yellow fever vaccine generally has few side effects; fewer than 5% of vaccinees develop mild headache, muscle pain, or other minor symptoms 5 to 10 days after vaccination. Under almost all circumstances, there are four groups of people who should not receive the vaccine unless the risk of yellow fever disease exceeds the small risk associated with the vaccine. These people should obtain either a waiver letter prior to travel or delay travel to an area with active yellow fever transmission:

- Yellow fever vaccine should never be given to infants under 6 months of age due to a risk of viral encephalitis developing in the child. In most cases, vaccination should be deferred until the child is 9 to 12 months of age.
- Pregnant women should not be vaccinated because of a theoretical risk that the developing fetus may become infected from the vaccine.
- Persons hypersensitive to eggs should not receive the vaccine because it is prepared in embryonated eggs. If vaccination of a traveler with a questionable history of egg hypersensitivity is considered essential, an intradermal test dose may be administered under close medical supervision. (Notify your doctor prior to vaccination if you think that you may be allergic to the vaccine or to egg products.)
- Persons with an immunosuppressed condition associated with AIDS or HIV infection, or those whose immune system has been altered by either diseases such as leukemia and lymphoma or through drugs and radiation should not receive the vaccine. People with asymptomatic HIV infection may be vaccinated if exposure to yellow fever cannot be avoided.

If you have one of these conditions, your doctor will be able to help you decide whether you should be vaccinated, delay your travel, or obtain a waiver. In all cases, the decision to immunize an infant between 6 and 9 months of age, a pregnant woman, or an immunocompromised patient should be made on an individual basis. The physician should weigh the risks of exposure and contracting the disease against the risks of immunization, and possibly consider alternative means of protection.

Medical Waivers

Most countries will accept a medical waiver for persons with a medical reason for not receiving the vaccination. CDC recommends obtaining written waivers from consular or embassy officials before departure. Travelers should contact the embassy or consulate for specific advice. Typically, a physician's letter stating the reason for withholding the vaccination and written on letterhead stationery is required by the embassy or consulate. The letter should bear the stamp used by a health department or official immunization center to validate the International Certificate of Vaccination.

Yellow fever vaccination requirements and recommendations for specific countries are available from the CDC Travelers' Health page.

Viral Hemorrhagic Fevers

(From http://www.cdc.gov/ncidod/dvrd/spb/mnpages/dispages/vhf.htm)

What Are Viral Hemorrhagic Fevers?

Viral hemorrhagic fevers (VHFs) refer to a group of illnesses that are caused by several distinct families of viruses. In general, the term "viral hemorrhagic fever" is used to describe a severe multi-system syndrome (multi-system in that multiple organ systems in the body are affected). Characteristically, the overall vascular system is damaged, and the body's ability to regulate itself is impaired. These symptoms are often accompanied by hemorrhage (bleeding); however, the bleeding is itself rarely life-threatening. While some types of hemorrhagic fever viruses can cause relatively mild illnesses, many of these viruses cause severe, life-threatening disease.

How Are Hemorrhagic Fever Viruses Grouped?

VHFs are caused by viruses of four distinct families: arenaviruses, filoviruses, bunyaviruses, and flaviviruses. Each of these families share a number of features:

- They are all RNA viruses, and all are covered, or enveloped, in a fatty (lipid) coating.
- Their survival is dependent on an animal or insect host, called the natural reservoir.
- The viruses are geographically restricted to the areas where their host species live.

- Humans are not the natural reservoir for any of these viruses. Humans are infected when they come into contact with infected hosts. However, with some viruses, after the accidental transmission from the host, humans can transmit the virus to one another.
- Human cases or outbreaks of hemorrhagic fevers caused by these viruses occur sporadically and irregularly. The occurrence of outbreaks cannot be easily predicted.
- With a few noteworthy exceptions, there is no cure or established drug treatment for VHFs.

In rare cases, other viral and bacterial infections can cause a hemorrhagic fever; scrub typhus is a good example.

What Carries Viruses That Cause Viral Hemorrhagic Fevers?

Viruses associated with most VHFs are zoonotic. This means that these viruses naturally reside in an animal reservoir host or arthropod vector. They are totally dependent on their hosts for replication and overall survival. For the most part, rodents and arthropods are the main reservoirs for viruses causing VHFs. The multimammate rat, cotton rat, deer mouse, house mouse, and other field rodents are examples of reservoir hosts. Arthropod ticks and mosquitoes serve as vectors for some of the illnesses. However, the hosts of some viruses remain unknown -- Ebola and Marburg viruses are well-known examples.

Where Are Cases of Viral Hemorrhagic Fever Found?

Taken together, the viruses that cause VHFs are distributed over much of the globe. However, because each virus is associated with one or more particular host species, the virus and the disease it causes are usually seen only where the host species live(s). Some hosts, such as the rodent species carrying several of the New World arenaviruses, live in geographically restricted areas. Therefore, the risk of getting VHFs caused by these viruses is restricted to those areas. Other hosts range over continents, such as the rodents that carry viruses which cause various forms of hantavirus pulmonary syndrome (HPS) in North and South America, or the different set of rodents that carry viruses which cause hemorrhagic fever with renal syndrome (HFRS) in Europe and Asia. A few hosts are distributed nearly worldwide, such as the common rat. It can carry Seoul virus, a cause of HFRS; therefore, humans can get HFRS anywhere where the common rat is found.

While people usually become infected only in areas where the host lives, occasionally people become infected by a host that has been exported from its native habitat. For example, the first outbreaks of Marburg hemorrhagic fever, in Marburg and Frankfurt, Germany, and in Yugoslavia, occurred when laboratory workers handled imported monkeys infected with Marburg virus. Occasionally, a person becomes infected in an area where the virus occurs naturally and then travels elsewhere. If the virus is a type that can be transmitted further by person-to-person contact, the traveler could infect other people. For instance, in 1996, a medical professional treating patients with Ebola hemorrhagic fever (Ebola HF) in Gabon unknowingly became infected. When he later traveled to South Africa and was treated for Ebola HF in a hospital, the virus was transmitted to a nurse. She became ill and died. Because more and more people travel each year, outbreaks of these diseases are becoming an increasing threat in places where they rarely, if ever, have been seen before.

How Are Hemorrhagic Fever Viruses Transmitted?

Viruses causing hemorrhagic fever are initially transmitted to humans when the activities of infected reservoir hosts or vectors and humans overlap. The viruses carried in rodent reservoirs are transmitted when humans have contact with urine, fecal matter, saliva, or other body excretions from infected rodents. The viruses associated with arthropod vectors are spread most often when the vector mosquito or tick bites a human, or when a human crushes a tick. However, some of these vectors may spread virus to animals, livestock, for example. Humans then become infected when they care for or slaughter the animals.

Some viruses that cause hemorrhagic fever can spread from one person to another, once an initial person has become infected. Ebola, Marburg, Lassa and Crimean-Congo hemorrhagic fever viruses are examples. This type of secondary transmission of the virus can occur directly, through close contact with infected people or their body fluids. It can also occur indirectly, through contact with objects contaminated with infected body fluids. For example, contaminated syringes and needles have played an important role in spreading infection in outbreaks of Ebola hemorrhagic fever and Lassa fever.

What Are the Symptoms of Viral Hemorrhagic Fever Illnesses?

Specific signs and symptoms vary by the type of VHF, but initial signs and symptoms often include marked fever, fatigue, dizziness, muscle aches, loss of strength, and exhaustion. Patients with severe cases of VHF often show signs of bleeding under the skin, in internal organs, or from body orifices like the mouth, eyes, or ears. However, although they may bleed from many sites around the body, patients rarely die because of blood loss. Severely ill patient cases may also show shock, nervous system malfunction, coma, delirium, and seizures. Some types of VHF are associated with renal (kidney) failure.

How Are Patients with Viral Hemorrhagic Fever Treated?

Patients receive supportive therapy, but generally speaking, there is no other approved treatment or established cure for VHFs. Treatment with convalescent-phase plasma has been used with success in some patients with Argentine hemorrhagic fever.

How Can Cases of Viral Hemorrhagic Fever Be Prevented and Controlled?

With the exception of yellow fever and Argentine hemorrhagic fever, for which vaccines have been developed (but not licensed in the U.S.), no vaccines exist that can protect against these diseases. Therefore, prevention efforts must concentrate on avoiding contact with host species. If prevention methods fail and a case of VHF does occur, efforts should focus on preventing further transmission from person to person, if the virus can be transmitted in this way. Because many of the hosts that carry hemorrhagic fever viruses are rodents, disease prevention efforts include:

- Controlling rodent populations;
- Discouraging rodents from entering or living in homes or workplaces; and
- Encouraging safe cleanup of rodent nests and droppings.

For hemorrhagic fever viruses spread by arthropod vectors, prevention efforts often focus on community-wide insect and arthropod control. In addition, people are encouraged to use insect repellant, proper clothing, bednets, window screens, and other insect barriers to avoid being bitten.

For those hemorrhagic fever viruses that can be transmitted from one person to another, avoiding close physical contact with infected people and their body fluids is the most important way of controlling the spread of disease. Barrier nursing or infection control techniques include isolating infected individuals and wearing protective clothing. Other infection control recommendations include proper use, disinfection, and disposal of instruments and equipment used in treating or caring for patients with VHF, such as needles and thermometers.

In conjunction with the World Health Organization, CDC has developed practical, hospital-based guidelines titled "Infection Control for Viral Haemorrhagic Fevers In the African Health Care Setting." The manual can help healthcare facilities recognize cases and prevent further hospital-based disease transmission using locally available materials and few financial resources.

Severe Acute Respiratory Syndrome (SARS)

(From http://www.cdc.gov/ncidod/sars/factsheet.htm)

SARS

Severe acute respiratory syndrome (SARS) is a viral respiratory illness caused by a coronavirus, called SARS-associated coronavirus (SARS-CoV). SARS was first reported in Asia in February 2003. Over the next few months, the illness spread to more than two dozen countries in North America, South America, Europe, and Asia before the SARS global outbreak of 2003 was contained. This fact sheet gives basic information about the illness and what CDC has done to control SARS in the United States.

The SARS Outbreak of 2003

According to the World Health Organization (WHO), a total of 8,098 people worldwide became sick with SARS during the 2003 outbreak. Of these, 774 died. In the United States, only eight people had laboratory evidence of SARS-CoV infection. All of these people had traveled to other parts of the world with SARS. SARS did not spread more widely in the community in the United States.

Symptoms of SARS

In general, SARS begins with a high fever (temperature greater than 100.4°F [>38.0°C]). Other symptoms may include headache, an overall feeling of discomfort, and body aches. Some people also have mild respiratory symptoms at the outset. About 10 percent to 20 percent of patients have diarrhea. After 2 to 7 days, SARS patients may develop a dry cough. Most patients develop pneumonia.

How SARS Spreads

The main way that SARS seems to spread is by close person-to-person contact. The virus that causes SARS is thought to be transmitted most readily by respiratory droplets (droplet spread) produced when an infected person coughs or sneezes. Droplet spread can happen when droplets from the cough or sneeze of an infected person are propelled a short distance (generally up to 3 feet) through the air and deposited on the mucous membranes of the mouth, nose, or eyes of persons who are nearby. The virus also can spread when a person touches a surface or object contaminated with infectious droplets and then touches his or her mouth, nose, or eye(s). In addition, it is possible that the SARS virus might spread more broadly through the air (airborne spread) or by other ways that are not now known.

What Does "Close Contact" Mean?

In the context of SARS, close contact means having cared for or lived with someone with SARS or having direct contact with respiratory secretions or body fluids of a patient with SARS. Examples of close contact include kissing or hugging, sharing eating or drinking utensils, talking to someone within 3 feet, and touching someone directly. Close contact does not include activities like walking by a person or briefly sitting across a waiting room or office.

CDC Response to SARS during the 2003 Outbreak

CDC worked closely with WHO and other partners in a global effort to address the SARS outbreak of 2003. For its part, CDC took the following actions:

- Activated its Emergency Operations Center to provide round-the-clock coordination and response.
- Committed more than 800 medical experts and support staff to work on the SARS response.
- Deployed medical officers, epidemiologists, and other specialists to assist with on-site investigations around the world.
- Provided assistance to state and local health departments in investigating possible cases of SARS in the United States.
- Conducted extensive laboratory testing of clinical specimens from SARS patients to identify the cause of the disease.

- Initiated a system for distributing health alert notices to travelers who may have been exposed to cases of SARS.

What CDC is Doing Now

CDC continues to work with other federal agencies, state and local health departments, and healthcare organizations to plan for rapid recognition and response if person-to-person transmission of SARS-CoV recurs. CDC has developed recommendations and guidelines to help public health and healthcare officials plan for and respond quickly to the reappearance of SARS in a healthcare facility or community. These are available in the document Public Health Guidance for Community-Level Preparedness and Response to Severe Acute Respiratory Syndrome (SARS). CDC provides the latest information on SARS on the SARS website.

Influenza*

(*Caused by novel or re-emergent influenza viruses that are causing, or have the potential to cause, a pandemic. From http://www.pandemicflu.gov/general/index.html.)

Pandemic Influenza

What's Happening Now?

A pandemic is a global disease outbreak. A flu pandemic occurs when a new influenza virus emerges for which people have little or no immunity, and for which there is no vaccine. The disease spreads easily person-to-person, causes serious illness, and can sweep across the country and around the world in very short time.

It is difficult to predict when the next influenza pandemic will occur or how severe it will be. Wherever and whenever a pandemic starts, everyone around the world is at risk. Countries might, through measures such as border closures and travel restrictions, delay arrival of the virus, but cannot stop it.

Health professionals are concerned that the continued spread of a highly pathogenic avian H5N1 virus across eastern Asia and other countries represents a significant threat to human health. The highly pathogenic H5N1 avian flu virus has raised concerns about a potential human pandemic because:

- It has proven to be transmitted from birds to mammals and, in some limited circumstances, to humans, and
- Like other influenza viruses, it continues to evolve and could develop greater affinity for human cells.

Since 2003, a growing number of human H5N1 cases have been reported in Azerbaijan, Cambodia, China, Djibouti, Egypt, Indonesia, Iraq, Thailand, Turkey, and Vietnam. More than half of the people infected with the H5N1 virus have died. Most of these cases are all believed to have been caused by exposure to infected poultry. There has been no sustained human-tohuman transmission of the disease, but the concern is that H5N1 will evolve into a virus capable of human-to-human transmission.

Avian Influenza Viruses

Avian (bird) flu is caused by influenza A viruses that occur naturally among birds. There are different subtypes of these viruses because of changes in certain proteins (hemagglutinin [HA] and neuraminidase [NA]) on the surface of the influenza A virus and the way the proteins combine.

Each combination represents a different subtype. All known subtypes of influenza A viruses can be found in birds. The avian flu currently of concern is a highly pathogenic H5N1 subtype.

Avian Influenza in Birds

Avian influenza is a virus that infects wild birds (such as ducks, gulls, and shorebirds) and domestic poultry (such as chickens, turkeys, ducks, and geese). AI strains are divided into two groups based upon the ability of the virus to produce disease in poultry: low pathogenic avian influenza (LPAI) and highly pathogenic avian influenza (HPAI).

LPAI, or "low path" avian influenza, naturally occurs in wild birds and can spread to domestic birds. In most cases it causes no signs of infection or only minor symptoms in birds. These strains of the virus pose little threat to human health. LPAI H5 and H7 strains have the potential to mutate into HPAI and are therefore closely monitored.

HPAI, or "high path" avian influenza, is often fatal in chickens and turkeys. HPAI spreads more rapidly than LPAI and has a higher death rate in birds. HPAI H5N1 is the type rapidly spreading in some parts of the world.

Wild birds worldwide carry avian influenza viruses in their intestines, but usually do not get sick from them. Infected birds shed influenza virus in their saliva, nasal secretions, and feces. Domesticated birds can become infected with avian influenza virus through direct contact with infected waterfowl or other infected poultry, or through contact with surfaces (such as dirt or cages) or materials (such as water or feed) that have been contaminated with the virus.

Human Infection with Avian Influenza Viruses

"Human influenza virus" usually refers to those subtypes that spread widely among humans. There are only three known A subtypes of influenza viruses (H1N1, H1N2, and H3N2) currently circulating among humans. It is likely that some genetic parts of current human influenza A viruses originally came from birds. Influenza A viruses are constantly changing, and other strains might adapt over time to infect and spread among humans.

The risk from avian influenza is generally low to most people, because the viruses do not usually infect humans. Highly pathogenic H5N1 is one of the few avian influenza viruses to have crossed the species barrier to infect humans, and it is the most deadly of those that have crossed the barrier.

Most cases of highly pathogenic H5N1 avian influenza infection in humans have resulted from contact with infected poultry (e.g., domesticated chicken, ducks, and turkeys) or surfaces contaminated with secretion/excretions from infected birds.

So far, the spread of highly pathogenic H5N1 avian influenza virus from person to person has been limited and has not continued beyond one person. Nonetheless, because all influenza viruses have the ability to change, scientists are concerned that the highly pathogenic H5N1 avian influenza virus circulating in Asia, Europe, and Africa one day could be able to infect humans and spread easily from one person to another.

In the current outbreaks in Asia, Europe, and Africa, more than half of those infected with the highly pathogenic H5N1 avian influenza virus have died. Most cases have occurred in previously healthy children and young adults. However, it is possible that the only cases currently being reported are those in the most severely ill people, and that the full range of illness caused by the highly pathogenic H5N1 avian influenza virus has not yet been defined.

Symptoms of avian influenza in humans have ranged from typical human influenza-like symptoms (e.g., fever, cough, sore throat, and muscle aches) to eye infections, pneumonia, severe respiratory diseases (such as acute respiratory distress), and other severe and life-threatening complications. The symptoms of avian influenza may depend on which virus caused the infection.

Because these viruses do not commonly infect humans, there is little or no immune protection against them in the human population. If the highly pathogenic H5N1 avian influenza virus were to gain the capacity to spread easily from person to person, a pandemic (worldwide outbreak of disease) could begin. No one can predict when a pandemic might occur. However, experts from around the world are watching the highly pathogenic H5N1 situation very closely and are preparing for the possibility that the virus may begin to spread more easily and widely from person to person.

For the most current information about avian influenza and cumulative case numbers, see the map on the CDC pandemic flu home page.

For more information about human infection, see http://www.cdc.gov/flu/avian/gen-info/avian-fluhumans.htm.

Vaccination and Treatment for H5N1 Virus in Humans

There currently is no commercially available vaccine to protect humans against H5N1 virus that is being seen in Asia, Europe, and Africa. Development is currently proceeding on pandemic vaccines based upon some already identified H5N1 strains.

The U.S. Department of Health and Human Services (HHS), through its National Institute of Allergy and Infectious Diseases (NIAID) and Food and Drug Administration, is addressing the problem in a number of ways. These include the development of pre-pandemic vaccines based on current lethal strains of H5N1, collaboration with industry to increase the Nation's vaccine production capacity, and seeking ways to expand or extend the existing supply. We are also doing research in the development of new types of influenza vaccines.

Studies done in laboratories suggest that some of the prescription medicines approved in the United States for human influenza viruses should work in treating avian influenza infection in humans. However, influenza viruses can become resistant to these drugs, so these medications may not always work. Additional studies are needed to demonstrate the effectiveness of these medicines.

The H5N1 virus that has caused human illness and death in Asia is resistant to amantadine and rimantadine, two antiviral medications commonly used for influenza. Two other antiviral medications, oseltamavir and zanamavir, would probably work to treat influenza caused by H5N1 virus, but additional studies still need to be done to demonstrate their effectiveness.

For more information about H5N1 drug and vaccine development, see http://www.pandemicflu.gov/vaccine/#research

What Would Be the Impact of a Pandemic?

A pandemic may come and go in waves, each of which can last for six to eight weeks. An especially severe influenza pandemic could lead to high levels of illness, death, social disruption, and economic loss. Everyday life would be disrupted because so many people in so many places become seriously ill at the same time. Impacts can range from school and business closings to the interruption of basic services such as public transportation and food delivery.

A substantial percentage of the world's population will require some form of medical care. Health care facilities can be overwhelmed, creating a shortage of hospital staff, beds, ventilators and other supplies. Surge capacity at non-traditional sites such as schools may need to be created to cope with demand.

The need for vaccine is likely to outstrip supply and the supply of antiviral drugs is also likely to be inadequate early in a pandemic. Difficult decisions will need to be made regarding who gets antiviral drugs and vaccines.

Death rates are determined by four factors: the number of people who become infected, the virulence of the virus, the underlying characteristics and vulnerability of affected populations and the availability and effectiveness of preventive measures.

How Are We Preparing?

The United States has been working closely with other countries and the World Health Organization (WHO) to strengthen systems to detect outbreaks of influenza that might cause a pandemic. See Global Activities

The effects of a pandemic can be lessened if preparations are made ahead of time. Planning and preparation information and checklists are being prepared for various sectors of society, including information for individuals and families. See Planning & Response Activities.

HHS and other federal agencies are providing funding, advice, and other support to your state to assist with pandemic planning and preparation. Information on state/federal planning and cooperation, including links to state pandemic plans, is available on this site. See State & Local Planning.

The federal government will provide up-to-date information and guidance to the public through the public media and this web site should an influenza pandemic unfold.

WHO Phases of a Pandemic

WHO has developed a global influenza preparedness plan, which defines the phases of a pandemic, outlines the role of WHO, and makes recommendations for national measures before and during a pandemic. The phases are:

Interpandemic Period

Phase 1: No new influenza virus subtypes have been detected in humans. An influenza virus subtype that has caused human infection may be present in animals. If present in animals, the risk of human infection or disease is considered to be low.

Phase 2: No new influenza virus subtypes have been detected in humans. However, a circulating animal influenza virus subtype poses a substantial risk of human disease.

Pandemic Alert Period

Phase 3: Human infection(s) with a new subtype, but no human-to-human spread, or at most rare instances of spread to a close contact.

Phase 4: Small cluster(s) with limited human-to-human transmission but spread is highly localized, suggesting that the virus is not well adapted to humans.

Phase 5: Larger cluster(s) but human-to-human spread still localized, suggesting that the virus is becoming increasingly better adapted to humans but may not yet be fully transmissible (substantial pandemic risk).

Pandemic Period

Phase 6: Pandemic: increased and sustained transmission in general population.

Notes:

- The distinction between **Phases 1** and **2** is based on the risk of human infection or disease resulting from circulating strains in animals. The distinction is based on various factors and their relative importance according to current scientific knowledge. Factors may include pathogenicity in animals and humans, occurrence in domesticated animals and livestock or only in wildlife, whether the virus is enzootic or epizootic, geographically localized or widespread, and other scientific parameters.
- The distinction among **Phases 3**, **4,** and **5** is based on an assessment of the risk of a pandemic. Various factors and their relative importance according to current scientific knowledge may be considered. Factors may include rate of transmission, geographical location and spread,

severity of illness, presence of genes from human strains (if derived from an animal strain), and other scientific parameters.

U.S. Government Stages of a Pandemic

The WHO phases provide succinct statements about the global risk for a pandemic and provide benchmarks against which to measure global response capabilities. In order to describe the U.S. government approach to the pandemic response, however, it is more useful to characterize the stages of an outbreak in terms of the immediate and specific threat a pandemic virus poses to the U.S. population. The following stages provide a framework for Federal Government actions:

Stage 0: New Domestic Animal Outbreak in Previously Unaffected Country (WHO Phase 3)

Stage 1: Suspected Human Outbreak Overseas (WHO Phase 3)

Stage 2: Confirmed Human Outbreak Overseas (WHO Phase 4 or 5)

Stage 3: Widespread Human Outbreaks in Multiple Locations Overseas (WHO Phase 6)

Stage 4: First Human Case in North America (WHO Phase 6)

Stage 5: Spread throughout United States (WHO Phase 6)

Stage 6: Recovery and Preparation for Subsequent Waves (WHO Phase 6 or 5)

APPENDIX G: AIRPORT QUARANTINE PLAN EXAMPLE

The following information was extracted with permission from:

State of Georgia
Division of Public Health Emergency Operations Plan
Incident Annex 3
Infectious Disease Evaluation and Response at
Hartsfield-Jackson International Airport
Standard Operating Plan
Version 20: May 25, 2006

Annex 1: Special Needs Population Shelter (SNPS*) Operations

(*Note: A list of abbreviations is provided on page G-11)

Appropriate PPE and separation of the travelers and response staff should be encouraged and utilized. Level of PPE will be determined by the potential infectious agent(s). May also need to consider the isolation of those travelers that had close contact with the index ill traveler and the ill traveler's close personal contacts/family members.

SNPS will be established upon the authority of the DIRECTOR DPH, when it has been determined the aircraft travelers will require quarantine. Services will be provided by the various support agencies listed in this Annex. The basic setup, physical layout, staffing and guidance for shelters are documented in the American Red Cross Shelter Manuals and the DPH "Guidelines for the Care of Special Needs Populations During Disasters and Emergencies". The following are recommended amenities, suggested by the planning committee.

This Annex is divided into 4 subsections: Accommodations, Administration, Special Travelers, and Supplies and Amenities.

Accommodations

The SNPS plan is complicated by potential international travelers and those deemed a high risk under the FBI's passenger classification system. If the quarantine is caused by a terrorist event, it may require a large number of people to receive vaccination and/or prophylaxis (VP), to protect the community at large from an infectious disease of public health concern and to allow the federal law enforcement agency in charge a more controlled environment to investigate travelers.

The SNPS should be a building located on the airport grounds, allowing better security and ease of transporting the travelers. The current primary site should be a hangar and the secondary site should be a nearby building with appropriate room and facilities. Some of the more obvious factors to be considered include external and internal security measures and rest room and shower facilities. The layout should be such that other amenities may be accommodated for staff and travelers.

If a hangar is to be used, then it should be capable of providing space for the unique requirements for this SNPS. On the runway side, the hangar doors open, allowing the nose of aircraft to enter the hangar. Having the travelers enter from the runway side protects them from the media, which may be located on the opposite side on the access road. The travelers will off load and register on the first floor, just inside the hangar doors. This allows the passengers and crew to be in a controlled access environment. Once in-processed, travelers will be escorted to the "residents" area. The restricted air access of the airport may limit the opportunity for the media to observe from the air.

Residents' Area:

The primary residents area should be a climate controlled large warehouse like area, capable of accommodating up to 400 residents in an open, but semi-private environment. Depending on contagiousness/infectiousness of the agent, portable negative pressure equipment with High Efficiency Particulate Air (HEPA) filtration might be recommended and requested through DHR EM. Sleeping arrangements (using current ARC shelter information as guidance) should provide space for families, couples and singles (adult and teenager). Separate areas should be set up for unforeseen events requiring separation of specific populations. Appropriate arrangements should be made for the care and supervision of unaccompanied children under 18 years old and accompanied and unaccompanied pets.

An area for washing non-contaminated clothes will be requested through OHS-GEMA. A company that deals with contaminated linens will be requested through OHS-GEMA to provide laundry services. The travelers may be responsible for housekeeping of their own residential area, but adequate supplies will be requested through OHS-GEMA.

A religious area should be established for the travelers to practice their religious beliefs. The area should accommodate religious services as requested by the travelers.

A respite area for travelers should be provided.

A separate secured area should be provided for visitation between the travelers, immediate families, counselors, other consultation services and media. There should be a solid, shatter-resistant window separating the visitors from the travelers, with adequate telephone-like systems for them to talk. There will be no access between the rooms; no physical contact between visitors and travelers. There will be controlled and escorted access into both rooms, not allowing any physical contact between visitors and travelers. It is strongly recommended to have a portable HEPA filtration system installed.

A recreational area should be provided, so the travelers can play games, such as basketball, or to walk.

A children's playroom should be provided. A television, games and other toys (age dependent) should be provided. There will be at least 2 (two) adult attendants at all times in the room (this could be staffed by the aircrew).

Staff Area:

The SNPS EOC will be the administrative center for the SNPS. The following representatives should be expected to staff the EOC: ARC; OHS-GEMA, DPH, DHR EM representative, DFCS, Regional Coordinating Hospital, airport management; FBI, GBI, Atlanta PD, CBP and other law enforcement agencies as required; airline representative; and CDC, HHS Regional Emergency Coordinator, DHS-FEMA with stations with telephone and internet access, if requested. There will be additional stations set up as required. A dedicated line to the SOC and DHR EOC should be available.

The SNPS Administrative offices will be located in close proximity to the SNPS EOC. This will be the office for the DHD and other SNPS-ACC administrators as necessary.

The SNPS staff should establish a conference room for daily briefs, updates, dignitary visits and other administrative meetings as required.

Separate respite and recreational areas should be provided. The SNPS staff will be provided a separate sleeping/living area. This will be important when the staff cannot leave for the duration of the quarantine or for extended times. Most likely, these areas will be cubicle-like areas with a cot and electrical outlets, affording minimal privacy.

A separate shower and rest room facility will be requested through OHS-GEMA, but the style is unknown (semi-private to dorm-like). A separate clothes-washing area will be established.

Housekeeping services and an area for washing non-contaminated clothes will be requested through OHS-GEMA for the staff area, including the EOC, clinic, etc. A company that deals with contaminated linens will be requested through OHS-GEMA to provide laundry services.

A communication system should be established throughout the SNPS for announcements originating from the EOC. A separate system should be established to communicate with the residential area.

The loading dock should be available for the SNPS staff at all times. Access will be limited to staff only.

Media will have a separate facility, but near the SNPS, if available. Media will have limited, escorted access to the passengers, crew and staff.

Administration

Residents:

Parents or legal guardians may request and be authorized access to the SNPS to be with unaccompanied children or adults with special needs. Upon access to the SNPS, they become part of the cohort group.

Access to translators needs to be available.

ARC will help establish and maintain a small canteen. DFCS will assist with staffing the canteen, as the ARC personnel are not authorized in the area with biologically infected or potentially infected passengers and crew. Food, beverages and snacks will be coordinated through both ARC and OHS-GEMA and available on a 24-hour basis. If staffing is a possibility, it will be requested through OHS-GEMA, but may have to be coordinated by the air crew members, accomplished by the travelers. The menu will be as diverse as possible, to meet the needs of those with special medical, religious oriented, and vegetarian diets. Alcohol is unauthorized.

Luggage will be "matched" and distributed to the passengers and crewmembers after appropriate clearance by CBP.

On board animals will be handled and coordinated through GA Department of Agriculture, US Department of Agriculture, US Fish and Wildlife, CDC, OHS-GEMA and/or DPH Veterinarian.

Staff:

A Unified Command Structure will be established, which is NIMS compliant and follows the Georgia Emergency Operations Plan (GEOP) and DPH EOP.

Personnel required to prepare and initially staff the SNPS will report within 90-120 minutes after alert. The SNPS will be prepared to in-process and house the travelers within 2 (two) hours after the arrival of staff. Assistance to set-up the shelter will be coordinated with OHS-GEMA. In the interim, the travelers will be held in a secluded and secured area until it is prepared.

Personnel who are critical to the initial operation may require law enforcement assistance to the rally point, due to the traffic congestion in the metro Atlanta area. This needs to be considered and coordinated through the on-scene commander. The airport will provide secured transportation to the SNPS for not only the passengers, but also the staff.

It is accepted not all of the volunteers to staff the SNPS may receive pre-VP. Therefore, they will be part of the group that will receive VP in the initial hours of the set up. For situations when VP is not available, PPE will be provided and used as directed.

ARC, DFCS, OHS-GEMA, DHR MHDDAD local Emergency Management Agencies (EMAs) and DPH will provide the SNPS support for the travelers during their quarantine; assisting with feeding and clothing of the travelers; assisting with family notification for those who are in quarantine; and assisting with any financial issues of the quarantined travelers. Donated foods, supplies, clothing, equipment, etc will be managed and coordinated through OHS-GEMA.

Primary law enforcement responsibility is Atlanta Police Department (APD). They will coordinate additional needs and requirements with other local law enforcement agencies and CBP. DHR DFCS will request APD, Airport Detachment, to provide and coordinate certified law enforcement personnel to be stationed outside and inside the SNPS facility. Those law enforcement personnel stationed inside the SNPS will provide protection against intrusion, enforce quarantine, protection of staff from travelers, travelers from violent travelers and other duties as requested from DHR DFCS and/or DPH. Appropriate VP and/or PPE will be determined by the Unified Command section for those working/entering the residential area.

The FBI, Immigration and Customs Enforcement (ICE) and GBI will coordinate their law enforcement investigations, working with the APD (Airport Division), the affected airline's security, TSA, CBP, airport security and other state and federal officials. Local law enforcement will ensure unimpeded transportation access to the MTF, assist with transportation of lab specimens to the State Public Health Laboratory and/or the CDC laboratory and with emergency transportation of additional support personnel as requested by the Public Health Staff through OHS-GEMA, Airport Operations or DHR EM.

If the SNPS is established due to a terrorist event, DHS-FEMA may establish a Regional Response Coordination Center (RRCC), assisting as requested or required. The many federal assets will be available through the RRCC, including ESF 6 and ESF 8.

American Red Cross (ARC) will assist with establishment of the SNPS—coordinating food, water, cots, and other supplies. ARC will also coordinate, register, and in-process travelers staying in the SNPS and assist with family communications.

DHR Emergency Manager (EM) will provide assistance as needed upon request from the SNPS operations.

DHR Division of Family and Children's Services (DFCS) staff will coordinate the setup, function and maintenance of the SNPS. DHR Manager of SNPS will have operational oversight responsibility for the SNPS. Aircrew members will assist DFCS staff with passenger relations, shelter operations, and the care and well being of the unaccompanied children.

DPH Public Information Officer (PIO) will coordinate with the Joint Information Center (JIC) or other established joint communication center, assuming the lead for disseminating the Public Health information. The DPH PIO will coordinate messages and communication strategies with counterparts in DHR, DPH, and other partner agencies in and outsides the JIC before releasing any information. The PIO will coordinate communications and ensure updates with the media and the residents in the SNPS.

DPH Emergency Preparedness Team (EPT) will assist the DHD EC/EPS in coordinating information flow between the MTF(s), SNPS and the DHR Emergency Operations Center (EOC), if activated. The EPT will assist the DHD and the District EC/EPS as requested. If the DHR EOC is not activated, the DHR EM will be notified of events and requirements within the SNPS-ACC.

DPH Epidemiology Branch will conduct surveillance among the residents of the SNPS and responders and apply infection control measures as needed. A major component of this surveillance is to identify those exposed individuals who become infected and therefore, require separate isolation facilities.

The **State Medical Epidemiologist** (SME) will recommend vaccination and chemoprophylaxis of exposed travelers, responders, and SNPS personnel as indicated. The SME will provide oversight of the epidemiologic response with in the SNPS, including surveillance, chart reviews and other surveillance as required.

A DHD EC or Emergency Preparedness Specialist (EPS), from the metro Atlanta District Health Director's offices, will assist the assigned DHD with oversight of the SNPS; assist in the SNPS EOC; coordinate as required with other district, state and federal entities; and assist upon other requests as needed.

Mental Health Services Staff will be assigned by Division of Mental Health Developmental Disabilities and Addictive Diseases (MHDDAD) and other disaster mental health providers throughout the entire response. Adequate communication needs to be assured to minimize levels of stress within the family. Mental Health teams may be required. The SNPS staff will work with Public Health, assessing and determining those residents and staff requiring intervention. It is advisable to have a member of each team be available for impromptu consultations. Mental Health members shall provide seminars for the residents and staff, educating them in ways to help deal with their stressful environment. Very few of the passengers and crew should require routine mental health care. For those that will require this type of care, appropriate intervention services and counseling will be available through the DHR Mental Health Services.

Credentialing:

A credentialing system will be instituted and assigned badges will be prominently displayed at all times while on the SNPS grounds and in the SNPS facility. Those agencies that have vests and specific uniforms, may wear them along with the supplied badge. The EOC personnel will determine who has access and their level of access:

- **Logistics** will be white on black with "LOGISTICS" and limited to the dock area, but may have limited access to the staff area, including the EOC, clinic, etc as required to provide assistance;
- **Medical** will be red on white with "MEDICAL" and access to all areas. DPH personnel will also wear the Public Health vests;
- **Administrative** will be yellow on light blue with "ADMIN" and access to all areas except clinic and ward;
- **EOC personnel** will be yellow on black with "EOC" and have access to all areas;
- **Law Enforcement** will be green on tan with "LE" and access to all areas.

Visitors to the grounds and facility will initially be limited to the media, city, local county, state, and /or federal officials and authorized family members. All visitors, regardless of prominence (political or otherwise), will be escorted. Administration and DPH PIO/RC will coordinate the escorts. Assigned badges will be prominently displayed at all times while on the SNPS grounds and in the SNPS facility:

- **Government officials** will be orange on white with "GOV", with limited escorted access to the non-travelers area and to any area that does not have infectious people.
- **Family members** will be white on orange with "GUEST", with limited escort access to the visitation area. It will be up to the senior medical provider and EOC staff if access will be granted to the medical ward to visit family.
- **Media** will be black on white with "MEDIA" and always escorted while in the SNPS and be limited to non-passenger/non-patient care areas unless received appropriate VP.

Special Travelers

If either the airlines or law enforcement have confirmed that a certified sex offender is part of the cohort group, that individual will be in a separate sleeping area. Additionally, sex offenders will not be allowed to have contact with any child under the age of 18 without at least one adult present. This is also true for prisoners in transit and other travelers of law enforcement interest. These individuals may be assigned constant surveillance.

Other considerations might include dignitaries, military personnel, people that are substance dependent and other persons of interest. Though too lengthy to be approached in this SOP, the UC staff will need to be aware of this consideration.

Supplies and Amenities

A secured, bonded area for storing travelers' personal items will be provided.

An entertainment room will be requested through OHS-GEMA with a television, VCR, possibly a DVD player and stereo.

An internet cafe-like room will be requested through OHS-GEMA. There will be internet connections for those with their private computers. There will be community computers for those without their computers. Printers will be available. This will allow business people to continue their work, students to maintain contact with their schools and to provide the opportunity for the passengers and crew to keep in touch with their families and friends.

A communication room will be requested through OHS-GEMA, with phones to accommodate the travelers, including phone setups for the hearing impaired. Fax machines will be provided. There should be free long distance for those without the funds or inability to pay the long distance fees.

Closing of Facility

In consultation with the SME, OHS-GEMA, DNR EPD, the EPA, and the owner of the location used, appropriate cleaning and decontamination of facility, resources and supplies will be accomplished. If this is not possible, these agencies will determine the appropriate demolition and disposal of the building. In addition, these agencies will determine the appropriate disposal of resources and supplies.

ANNEX 2: SPECIAL NEEDS POPULATION SHELTER/ALTERNATE CARE CENTER

If possible, the ill, exposed or infectious traveler will be treated in a local medical treatment facility, capable to evaluate and treat the traveler.

An ill traveler will not be transported to a local medical treatment facility without due consideration of the agent or disease that initiated the quarantine. Prior to transfer, the health care provider seeing the ill traveler, should consult with the receiving medical treatment facility. Grady EMS or other similarly equipped and trained patient transport unit need to be notified and requested through the Airport Rescue and Fire Fighting. The health care provider should also consult with the SME, the lead DHD over seeing the SNSP/ACC, and if necessary, the DPH DIRECTOR, ensuring there is no or acceptable Public Health risk to the receiving MTF and others in contact with the traveler.

If it is determined the ill travelers should not be transported, evaluated nor admitted to a local medical treatment facility, then this ANNEX 2 will assist in the establishment of an ACC.

Due to the complexity of the sheltering and medical care issues, the quarantine facility will be designated as an SNPS. Within the SNPS, an ACC may be established. The ACC may be set up as minimally as an outpatient clinic or as complex as an inpatient facility. DPH will provide oversight and logistical coordination of personnel and supplies. DPH will coordinate with the DHD SNPS Director the medical oversight of the DHR SNPS-ACC. The Atlanta Region's Metropolitan Medical Response System's (MMRS)

Metropolitan Medical Strike Team (MMST) may assist DPH in setting up and staffing a clinic or inpatient facility, if required or requested by the SME or DIRECTOR DPH.

Administration

A Unified Command Structure will be established, which is NIMS compliant and follows the Georgia Emergency Operations Plan (GEOP) and DPH EOP.

HHS REC will work with other HHS Operating Divisions (OPDIVs) to coordinate the Emergency Support Function #8 (ESF #8) Health and Medical Response. Working with our partner agencies (NDMS, VA, and DoD) we will provide public health-related information regarding the cause of the event, and treat exposed individuals as well.

DHS-FEMA's NDMS Section ECs are responsible for coordinating NDMS activities, including DMAT, DMORT, etc.

DHR Emergency Manager (EM) will provide assistance as needed upon request from the SNPS ACC operations.

The **State Public Health Laboratory (PHL)** will assist the ACC medical staff with appropriate resources to provide laboratory testing. Some testing may need to be coordinated between the senior medical provider and the Director PHL. Laboratory results will be communicated to the senior medical provider or designee.

DPH Office of Pharmacy will assist the MMST and DMAT with pharmaceutical personnel and supply issues. OHS-GEMA, the Department of Homeland Security's Emergency Coordinators (DHS-ECs) and the Department of Health and Human Services Regional Emergency Coordinator (HHS-REC) may assist with obtaining personnel and supplies not available through the DPH Office of Pharmacy system.

DPH Public Information Officer (PIO) will coordinate with the Joint Information Center (JIC) or other established joint communication center, assuming the lead for disseminating the Public Health information. The DPH PIO will coordinate messages and communication strategies with counterparts in DHR, DPH, and other partner agencies in and outside the JIC before releasing any information. The PIO will coordinate communications and ensure updates with the media and the residents in the SNPS ACC.

DPH Emergency Preparedness Team (EPT) will assist the DHD EPS/EC in coordinating information flow between the MTF(s), SNPS ACC and the DHR Emergency Operations Center (EOC), if activated. The EPT will assist the DHD and the District EC/EPS as requested. If the DHR EOC is not activated, the DHR EM will be notified of events and requirements within the SNPS ACC.

DPH Epidemiology Branch will conduct surveillance among the patients and staff of the ACC and apply infection control measures as needed. The SME will provide oversight of the epidemiologic response within the ACC, including surveillance, chart reviews and other surveillance as required.

A DHD EC or Emergency Preparedness Specialist (EPS), from the metro Atlanta District Health Director's offices, will assist the assigned DHD with oversight of the SNPS ACC; and assist upon other requests as needed.

Physician and Nurse Staff will be assigned to the ACC from resources such as GA Disaster Medical Assistance Team (DMAT), MMST, GA Nurse Alert System (GNAS), GA Pharmacy Alert System (GPhAS), Georgia State Defense Force and/or other resources as provided by DPH and OHS-GEMA. The senior medical provider or designee will liaison with the Primary MTF for transported patients.

Mental Health Services Staff will be assigned by MHDDAD providers and other disaster mental health providers throughout the entire response. Adequate communication needs to be assured to minimize levels of stress within the staff. Mental health teams may be required. The ACC staff will work with Public Health, assessing and determining those patients and staff requiring intervention. It is advisable to have a member of each team be available for impromptu consultations. Mental health team members shall provide appropriate interventions for the patients and staff to help deal with their stressful environment. For patients with substance dependency, MHDDAD providers will assess need and appropriate treatment.

Radiological Services (diagnostic) may be coordinated with the MTFs, if the service is not available through the MMST or DMAT. The MMST and/or DMAT may request radiological assistance through the DPH. DPH may request assistance from DHS-ECs and HHS-REC.

Medical Operations

The medical situation of the SNPS ACC may lead to altered standards of medical care for the residents and staff. The altered standards of medical care have to be evaluated and approved or waived by the DIRECTOR DPH, in consultation with DHR Legal Services, OHS-GEMA, Governor, Georgia Hospital Association (GHA) and/or other agencies as determined.

Due to the probable infectious nature of their exposure, all travelers and staff will be treated, to the extent possible, in the ACC. Medical staff will consult with the SME if transport to an MTF is being considered. In the event of exhausting existing healthcare system, a small inpatient unit may need to be established to care for those that may require an inpatient-like setting. If an inpatient-like setting becomes necessary, it will be placed as to prevent cross exposure of staff and exposed residents.

Outpatient ACC

This is defined as the area within the SNPS facility that cares for staff and residents requiring routine medical care, unrelated to the exposure, similar to a small outpatient clinic or urgent care clinic. Clinical services, including mental health, radiology and prescription medication dispensing, including refills, will be coordinated through DPH. Staffing suggestions are covered later in this document.

Ill residents and staff may be transported to an MTF if the required scope of care exceeds that of the clinic or if the resident or staff develops symptoms consistent with the disease or agent exposure. The EMS transport unit of choice is the Grady Biosafety Transport Unit.

Inpatient ACC

If the area healthcare system can no longer provide needed isolation and treatment standards and if directed by the DPH DIRECTOR, OHS-GEMA, CDC, DHS or other authoritative agency/legislative body (state and/or federal), the ACC may be required to be staffed and equipped to provide inpatient care to ill residents and staff.

Necessary medical resources may need to be procured through the Metropolitan Medical Response System (MMRS). If unsuccessful, the DPH may request the resources through OHSGEMA.

The medical and nursing care will be performed by personnel appropriately trained and qualified to operate in an austere environment. If federal medical resources are required, they will be requested through OHS-GEMA.

Disposal of potentially infectious waste, linens, clothing and bedding will need to be recommended through the DPH Epidemiology and coordinated through DPH Environmental Health and OHS-GEMA.

Discharge planning for all residents and staff of the SNPS will be coordinated through the SME, in consultation with the DPH DIRECTOR.

General Staffing of the ACC

Separate inpatient and outpatient staffing arrangements should be considered and arranged whenever possible. Staffing requests will be made from DPH to HHS REC, OHS-GEMA or the Regional Coordinating Hospital, if required. The initial staffing requests should be made for either a DMAT or GSDF. Staffing ratio suggestion is based on the DoD Medical Emergency Modular System (MEMS) models, which is based on a 10 (ten) bed unit, with increments of 10 (ten), the following is recommended for staffing this ACC per 12 (twelve) hour shift:

- **Two physicians** (one responsible for the outpatient and one for inpatient care)
- **Two Physician's Assistants (PA) or Nurse Practitioners (NP)** (one assist with outpatient and one assist with inpatient care)
- **One Pharmacist** (responsible for the ACC; more would be assigned as the situation warrants)
- **One Pharmacy Technician**
- **Four nurses**; mix of Registered Nurses (RNs) and Licensed Practical Nurses (LPNs) (one RN to have oversight of the inpatient and one to oversee the outpatient care; one LPN to assist in the outpatient and one if an inpatient component exists)
- **Two nursing assistants** (to assist with inpatient care)
- **One medical unit secretary (responsible for the ACC)**
- **Two housekeepers** (one for outpatient care and one per 25 inpatient care)

(Reference DoD's MEMS)

ABBREVIATIONS AND ACRONYMS

ACC-Alternate Care Center
ARC-American Red Cross
AFCEMA-Atlanta Fulton County Emergency Management Agency
BT-Bioterrorism

BT/EC-Bioterrorism/Emergency Coordinator
CDC-Centers for Disease Control and Prevention
DFCS-Division of Family and Children's Services
DHD-District Health Director
DHR-Department of Human Resources
DHR EM-Department of Human Resources Emergency Management
DHS-FEMA- Department of Homeland Security-Federal Emergency Management Agency
DHS EC-Department of Homeland Security Emergency Coordinator
DMAT-Disaster Medical Assistance Team
DoD-Department of Defense
DPH-Division of Public Health
EC-Emergency Coordinator
ED-Emergency Department
EM-Electron Microscope
EMA-Emergency Management Agency
EMS-Emergency Medical Service
EOC-Emergency Operations Center
EPS- Emergency Preparedness Specialist
EPT-Emergency Preparedness Team
ERT-A-Emergency Response Team-Advanced
FBI SAIC-Federal Bureau of Investigation Special Agent In Charge
GA HLS-Georgia Homeland Security
GBI-Georgia Bureau of Investigation
GISAC-Georgia Information Sharing and Analysis Center
HLS-Homeland Security (Federal)
MTF-Medical Treatment Facility
MHDDAD
MMRS-Metropolitan Medical Response System
MMST-Metropolitan Medical Strike Team
OCGA-Official Code of Georgia Annotated
OHS-GEMA- Georgia Emergency Management Agency
NP- Nurse Practioner
PA- Physician Assistant
PAO-Public Affairs Officer
PIO
PCR-Polymerase Chain Reaction
PHL-Public Health Laboratory
PFO-Principal Federal Official

RC-Risk Communicator
SPX-Smallpox
SNPS-Special Needs Population Shelter
SNS-Strategic National Stockpile
SME-State Medical Epidemiologist
SOC-State Operations Center
VP-Vaccination and/or prophylaxis

APPENDIX H: INCIDENT COMMAND/UNIFIED COMMAND

Incident Command

[From the U.S. Department of Labor, Occupational Safety and Health Administration, http://www.osha.gov/SLTC/etools/ics/what is ics.html]

The ICS is a standardized on-scene incident management concept designed specifically to allow responders to adopt an integrated organizational structure equal to the complexity and demands of any single incident or multiple incidents without being hindered by jurisdictional boundaries.

In 1980, federal officials transitioned ICS into a national program called the National Interagency Incident Management System (NIIMS) (now known as the National Incident Management System [NIMS]), which became the basis of a response management system for all federal agencies with wildfire management responsibilities. Since then, many federal agencies have endorsed the use of ICS and several have mandated its use.

An ICS enables integrated communication and planning by establishing a manageable span of control. An ICS divides an emergency response into five manageable functions essential for emergency response operations: command, operations, planning, logistics, and finance and administration. Figure 1 below shows a typical ICS structure.

The **Incident Commander** (IC) or the **Unified Command** (UC) is responsible for all aspects of the response, including developing incident objectives and managing all incident operations.

The IC is faced with many responsibilities when he/she arrives on scene. Unless specifically assigned to another member of the Command or General Staffs, these responsibilities remain with the IC. Some of the more complex responsibilities include:

- Establish immediate priorities especially the safety of responders, other emergency workers, bystanders, and people involved in the incident.
- Stabilize the incident by ensuring life safety and managing resources efficiently and cost effectively.

Determine incident objectives and strategy to achieve the objectives.

- Establish and monitor incident organization.
- Approve the implementation of the written or oral Incident Action Plan (IAP).
- Ensure adequate health and safety measures are in place.

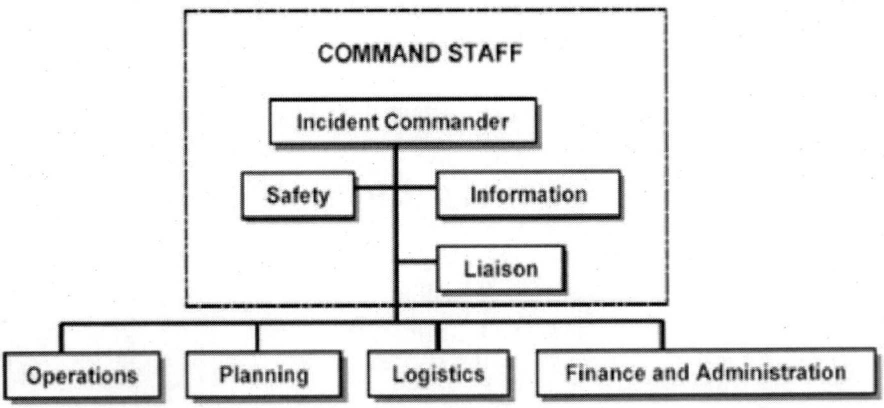

Figure 1. Incident Command System Structure.

The **Command Staff** is responsible for public affairs, health and safety, and liaison activities within the incident command structure. The IC/UC remains responsible for these activities or may assign individuals to carry out these responsibilities and report directly to the IC/UC.

- The **Information Officer's** role is to develop and release information about the incident to the news media, incident personnel, and other appropriate agencies and organizations.
- The **Liaison Officer's** role is to serve as the point of contact for assisting and coordinating activities between the IC/UC and various agencies and groups. This may include Congressional personnel, local

government officials, and criminal investigating organizations and investigators arriving on the scene.

- The **Safety Officer's** role is to develop and recommend measures to the IC/UC for assuring personnel health and safety and to assess and/or anticipate hazardous and unsafe situations. The Safety Officer also develops the Site Safety Plan, reviews the Incident Action Plan for safety implications, and provides timely, complete, specific, and accurate assessment of hazards and required controls.

The **General Staff** includes Operations, Planning, Logistics, and Finance/Administrative responsibilities. These responsibilities remain with the IC until they are assigned to another individual. When the Operations, Planning, Logistics or Finance/Administrative responsibilities are established as separate functions under the IC, they are managed by a section chief and can be supported by other functional units.

- The **Operations Staff** is responsible for all operations directly applicable to the primary mission of the response.
- The **Planning Staff** is responsible for collecting, evaluating, and disseminating the tactical information related to the incident, and for preparing and documenting IAPs.
- The **Logistics Staff** is responsible for providing facilities, services, and materials for the incident response.
- The **Finance and Administrative Staff** is responsible for all financial, administrative, and cost analysis aspects of the incident.

The following is a list of Command Staff and General Staff responsibilities that either the IC or UC of any response should perform or assign to appropriate members of the Command or General Staffs:

- Provide response direction;
- Coordinate effective communication;
- Coordinate resources;
- Establish incident priorities;
- Develop mutually agreed-upon incident objectives and approve response strategies;
- Assign objectives to the response structure;
- Review and approve IAPs;

- Ensure integration of response organizations into the ICS/UC;
- Establish protocols;
- Ensure worker and public health and safety; and
- Inform the media.

The modular organization of the ICS allows responders to scale their efforts and apply the parts of the ICS structure that best meet the demands of the incident. In other words, there are no hard and fast rules for when or how to expand the ICS organization. Many incidents will never require the activation of Planning, Logistics, or Finance/Administration Sections, while others will require some or all of them to be established. A major advantage of the ICS organization is the ability to fill only those parts of the organization that are required. For some incidents, and in some applications, only a few of the organization's functional elements may be required. However, if there is a need to expand the organization, additional positions exist within the ICS framework to meet virtually any need.

For example, in responses involving responders from a single jurisdiction, the ICS establishes an organization for comprehensive response management. However, when an incident involves more than one agency or jurisdiction, responders can expand the ICS framework to address a multi-jurisdictional incident.

The roles of the ICS participants will also vary depending on the incident and may even vary during the same incident. Staffing considerations are based on the needs of the incident. The number of personnel and the organization structure are dependent on the size and complexity of the incident. There is no absolute standard to follow. However, large-scale incidents will usually require that each component, or section, is set up separately with different staff members managing each section. A basic operating guideline is that the Incident Commander is responsible for all activities until command authority is transferred to another person.

Another key aspect of an ICS that warrants mention is the development of an IAP. A planning cycle is typically established by the Incident Commander and Planning Section Chief, and an IAP is then developed by the Planning Section for the next operational period (usually 12- or 24- hours in length) and submitted to the Incident Commander for approval. Creation of a planning cycle and development of an IAP for a particular operational period help focus available resources on the highest priorities/incident objectives. The planning cycle, if properly practiced, brings together everyone's input and identifies critical shortfalls that need to be addressed to carry out the Incident Commander's objectives for that period.

Unified Command (UC)

(From U.S. Department of Labor, Occupational Safety and Health Administration, http://www.osha.gov/SLTC/etools/ics/what is uc.html.]

Although a single Incident Commander normally handles the command function, an ICS organization may be expanded into a Unified Command (UC). The UC is a structure that brings together the "Incident Commanders" of all major organizations involved in the incident in order to coordinate an effective response while at the same time carrying out their own jurisdictional responsibilities. The UC links the organizations responding to the incident and provides a forum for these entities to make consensus decisions. Under the UC, the various jurisdictions and/or agencies and non-government responders may blend together throughout the operation to create an integrated response team.

The UC is responsible for overall management of the incident. The UC directs incident activities, including development and implementation of overall objectives and strategies, and approves ordering and releasing of resources. Members of the UC work together to develop a common set of incident objectives and strategies, share information, maximize the use of available resources, and enhance the efficiency of the individual response organizations.

The UC may be used whenever multiple jurisdictions are involved in a response effort. These jurisdictions could be represented by:

- Geographic boundaries (such as two states, Indian Tribal Land);
- Governmental levels (such as local, state, federal);
- Functional responsibilities (such as fire fighting, oil spill, Emergency Medical Services (EMS));
- Statutory responsibilities [such as federal land or resource managers, responsible party under the Oil Pollution Act of 1990 (OPA) or the Comprehensive Environmental Response, Compensation, and Liability Act (CERCLA)]; or
- Some combination of the above.

Actual UC makeup for a specific incident will be determined on a case-by-case basis taking into account: (1) the specifics of the incident; (2) determinations outlined in existing response plans; or (3) decisions reached during the initial meeting of the UC. The makeup of the UC may change as an incident progresses, in order to account for changes in the situation. The UC is a team effort, but to be effective, the number of personnel should be kept as small as possible.

Frequently, the first responders to arrive at the scene of an incident are emergency response personnel from local fire and police departments. The majority of local responders are familiar with National Incident Management System (NIMS) ICS and are likely to establish one immediately. As local, state, federal, and private party responders arrive on-scene for multi-jurisdictional incidents, responders would integrate into the ICS organization and establish a UC to direct the expanded organization. Although the role of local and state responders can vary depending on state laws and practices, local responders will usually be part of the ICS/UC.

Members in the UC have decision-making authority for the response. To be considered for inclusion as a UC representative, the representative's organization must:

- Have jurisdictional authority or functional responsibility under a law or ordinance for the incident;
- Have an area of responsibility that is affected by the incident or response operations;
- Be specifically charged with commanding, coordinating, or managing a major aspect of the response; and
- Have the resources to support participation in the response organization.

The addition of a UC to the ICS enables responders to carry out their own responsibilities while working cooperatively within one response management system. Under the National Contingency Plan (NCP), the UC may consist of a pre-designated On-Scene Coordinator (OSC), the state OSC, the Incident Commander for the Responsible Party (RP), and the local emergency response Incident Commander.

(The following page shows an example of an international airport UC structure.)

Unified Command Flowchart Example

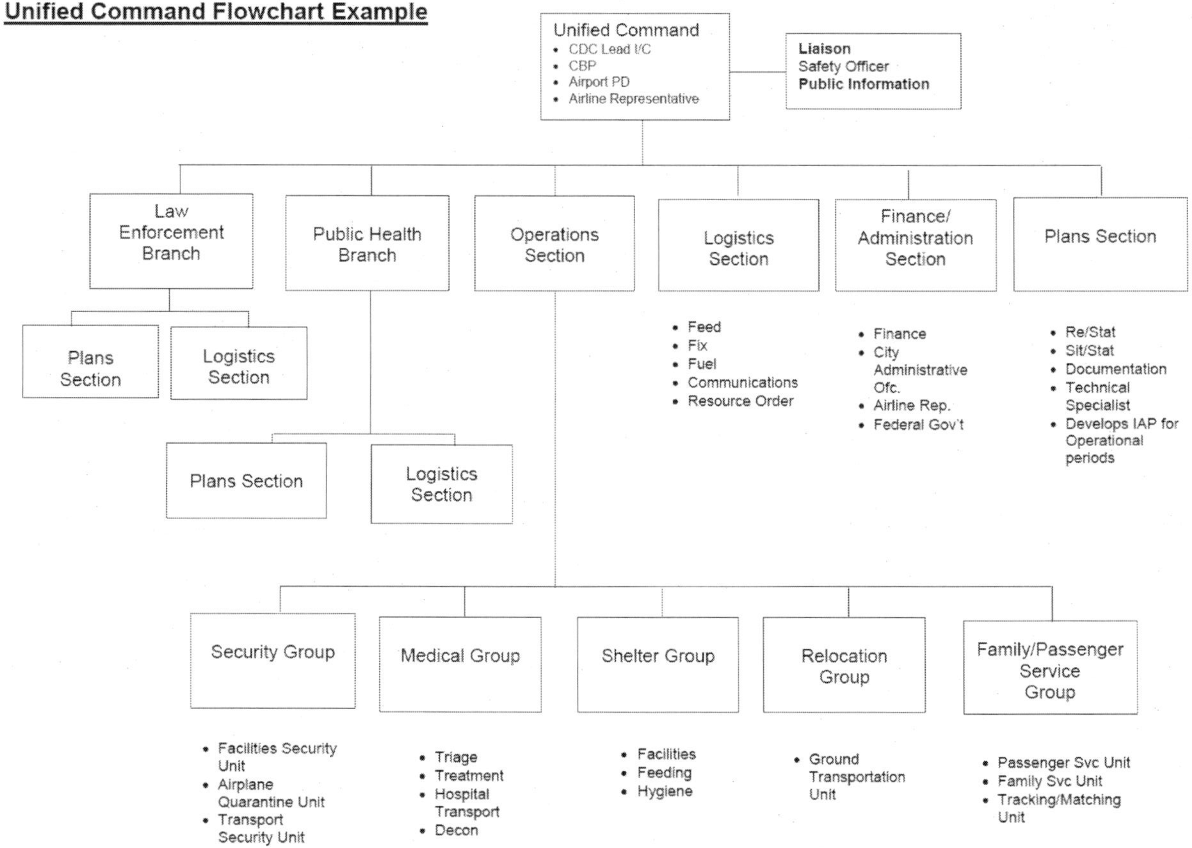

APPENDIX I: ABBREVIATIONS

APHIS	Animal and Plant Health Inspection Service
APIS	Advance Passenger Information System
CBP	U.S. Customs and Border Protection
CDC	Centers for Disease Control and Prevention
CFR	U.S. Code of Federal Regulations
DGMQ	CDC Division of Global Migration and Quarantine
DHS	Department of Homeland Security
DOT	U.S. Department of Transportation
eAPIS	Electronic Advance Passenger Information System
EMS	Emergency Medical Services
FAA	Federal Aviation Administration
FBI	Federal Bureau of Investigation
FEMA	Federal Emergency Management Agency
FWS	U.S. Fish and Wildlife Service
GOARN	Global Outbreak and Response Network
GPHIN	Global Public Health Intelligence Network
HAN	Health Alert Network/Health Alert Notice
HHS	Department of Health and Human Services
IC	Incident Command
ICS	Incident Command System
JIC	Joint Information Center
MOA	Memorandum of Agreement
MOU	Memorandum of Understanding
NIMS	National Incident Management System
NRP	National Response Plan
OSHA	Occupational Safety and Health Administration
PPE	Personal Protective Equipment
SARS	Severe Acute Respiratory Syndrome
TB	Tuberculosis
TSA	Transportation Security Administration
UC	Unified Command
USDA	U.S. Department of Agriculture
UTL	Universal Task List
WHO	World Health Organization

APPENDIX J: ACKNOWLEDGMENTS

Acknowledgments

Individuals and groups from the agencies and organizations listed below contributed to this Manual by providing critical information, contacts, input, commentary, or critical review.

Federal Government

- Department of Agriculture
- Department of Commerce
- Department of Energy
  - Oak Ridge Institute for Science and Education
- Department of Health and Human Services
  - Centers for Disease Control and Prevention
    - Division of Global Migration and Quarantine
      - Atlanta Quarantine Station
      - Boston Quarantine Station
      - Chicago Quarantine Station
      - Honolulu Quarantine Station
      - Houston Quarantine Station
      - Los Angeles Quarantine Station
      - New York Quarantine Station
      - San Francisco Quarantine Station
      - Seattle Quarantine Station
      - Washington Quarantine Station
    - Division of Healthcare Quality Promotion
  - Food and Drug Administration
- Department of Homeland Security
  - Customs and Border Protection
  - Immigration and Customs Enforcement
  - Office of Policy Development
  - Transportation Security Administration
- Department of Justice
  - Federal Bureau of Investigation
- Department of Labor
  - Occupational Safety and Health Administration
- Department of Transportation

  - Federal Aviation Administration
  - Office of the Secretary of Transportation
- Executive Office of the President
  - Office of Management and Budget
  - White House Homeland Security Council

State, Local, and Territorial Governments

- California
  - Los Angeles Fire Department
  - California Department of Health
- Virginia
  - Fairfax County Attorney's Office
- Washington
  - Washington Department of Health
- Guam Customs and Quarantine Agency

International

- Commission to Investigate the Introduction and Spread of SARS in Ontario and Toronto, Canada
- The Canadian Red Cross Society

United Nations

- International Civil Aviation Organization (ICAO)

Professional/Trade Organizations

- Airports Council International-North America (ACI-NA)
- Air Transport Association (ATA)
- Council of State and Territorial Epidemiologists (CSTE)
- International Air Transport Association (IATA)
- National Air Carrier Association (NACA)

Air Industry

- Airlines
  - Delta Airlines
  - Lufthansa
  - Northwest Airlines
  - United Airlines

- Airports
    - Atlanta Hartsfield Airport
    - Singapore Changi Airport (Taiwan)
    - Lester B. Pearson International Airport (Toronto)
    - Honolulu International Airport
    - John F. Kennedy International Airport
    - Seattle-Tacoma International Airport
- Airport Operators
    - Greater Toronto Airports Authority
    - Los Angeles World Airports
    - The Port Authority of New York and New Jersey
    - Miami-Dade Aviation Department (Florida)

INDEX

2

A

D

J

K

L

M

Q

R

S

T

U

V

W

Y